The Zen of Tennis

NANCY KORAN

Illustrations by Carl Anders Aabo
Foreword by Colin S. Dibley

Typesetting and graphic design by George Struk, Desktop Express, Glendale, NY

To

my beloved parents,

the Korans and the Glicksteins,

and

my precious husband, Steven

Acknowledgments

Special commemoration to my dear friend Billy Talbert, who was a paragon of etiquette and has enriched my life and the lives of others in so many ways on the court as well as off.

Eternal gratitude to my friend Colin Dibley, who has been so influential in the development of my book.

Heartfelt thanks to all the tennis stars and the celebrities who have personally contributed to this book. You are among the very best role models society has because of your commitment to helping others and because of the integrity with which you live your lives.

The tennis stars: Pauline Betz Addie, Vic Braden, Don Budge, Rosie Casals, Ross Case, Louise Brough Clapp, Ashley Cooper, Owen Davidson, Colin Dibley, Cliff Drysdale, Margaret Osborne duPont, Jo Durie, Neale Fraser, Shirley Fry-Irvin, Zina Garrison, Andres Gomez, Evonne Goolagong, Tom Gullikson, Doris Hart, Gladys M. Heldman, Jan Kodes, Rod Laver, Gene Mayer, Tim Mayotte, Frew McMillan, Angela Mortimer, Betsy Nagelsen, John Newcombe, Charles M. Pasarell, Jr., Jim Pugh, Ken Rosewall, Frank Sedgman, Pancho Segura, Vic Seixas, Pam Shriver, Stan Smith, Dick Stockton, Helena Sukova, Billy Talbert, Tony Trabert and Wendy Turnbull.

The celebrities: Steve Allen, Nick Bollettieri, Peter Burwash, Bud Collins, Tim Conway, Robert Goulet, Dina Merrill, George Michael, Regis Philbin, Ann Reinking, Kenny Rogers, Mickey Spillane, John Sterling, Oliver Stone and Adam West.

Immeasurable gratitude to all my tennis clients for the many happy memories we have shared on the court and for inspiring me to write this book.

To Mark Young and the Tennis Hall of Fame, I wish to express my deep appreciation for their patience and assistance throughout the process of writing this book.

Grateful recognition for their advice and assistance: Brenda Creswell, Joyce Stoudermire, Chaya Shimron, Jane Nichols, Steven Abramson, Jean Booth, Bernard Chase, Stefanie Robbins, Willie Chu, Nellie Sabin, Williamson L. Henderson, Vicki de Vries, Sandra Taylor, Sharon Klingler, Steve Harrison, Jean Detiere, Holly Irwin and Eileen Davis.

Special thanks to George Struk for his good humor and creative graphic design.

Infinite thanks to my public relations agent Sherri Rosen for her patience and devotion.

Finally, special acknowledgment to Charlie Aabo for taking my stick figures and turning them into masterpieces.

About the Cartoonist

Carl Anders Aabo was born and raised in the city of Stavanger, Norway. After completing mandatory military service in his native Norway, he worked for five years at the Professional Children's Theater in Stavanger.

Soon after moving to the United States, Carl enrolled at the Joe Kubert School of Cartooning and Graphic Art. Since his graduation, Carl's professional work has been in various related media, including children's books, animation and theater poster illustration.

An avid tennis player, he enjoys winning some of the time.

About the Author

Nancy Koran entered the world of tournament tennis at age 11, just six months after holding her first racquet. Facing competition from opponents, many of whom had begun playing the game as young as age four, showed Nancy the extent of the "catching up" she had to do in order to become proficient.

Numerous lessons with several well-known instructors, in addition to countless practice sessions with her father, cultivated her playing ability.

After playing junior tennis for seven years and attaining a national amateur ranking, Nancy earned a full scholarship to Ohio State University. After her graduation with a Bachelor of Arts degree in Communications, she ventured onto the women's tennis circuit.

Upon returning to her home in Silver Spring, Maryland, she was deluged with requests for tennis lessons from people interested in benefiting from her expertise. Nancy soon launched her successful tennis-teaching career, which extended seasonally from Palm Beach to the Hamptons. Nancy presently enjoys giving tennis lessons year-round in New York City.

The information in this text is a compilation of actual tennis experiences that Nancy and fellow tennis professionals have encountered while playing domestically and throughout the world.

Contents

Praise for *The Zen of Tennis*

Your book reminds me that etiquette counts. Sometimes I have trouble remembering that. I hardly ever jump over the net to congratulate someone who has just beaten my brains out. And sometimes I cannot muster up a sincere handshake. Now after reading *The Zen of Tennis*, I'll try harder, but I'd better win once in a while!

> Regis Philbin
> *Television Talk Show Host*

This is a nicely presented guide to tennis matters and is, in its larger sense, a call for courtesy in all matters human.

> Oliver Stone
> *Academy Award-winning Director, Producer, Writer and Actor*

Nancy's book has the answer to every etiquette question that you ever had about playing tennis, but were too intimidated to ask.

> George Michael
> *Sports Analyst and Commentator*

Absolutely great! It reminds me of why tennis should be fun!

> Mickey Spillane
> *Writer of mystery and detective novels, short stories, books for children, comic books and television/film scripts, and Producer*

Competition may be hot, but keeping your head and maintaining an agreeable level of sportsmanship and behavior are "cool" and make you feel good about yourself.

I have proved this to myself on a few occasions. The most deplorable occurred in a tournament when I was perturbed at myself for blowing a point. I hurled my racquet, a "steelie," over a fence. It then alighted on a parking lot, bounced and struck a man exiting in his auto. The poor fellow looked as though he had been hit by a small UFO.

As my embarrassed partner glowered and our opponents giggled, I had to leave the court, retrieve the racquet and apologize to the unhurt victim, all the while hoping that he wasn't a lawyer. That is why I do not throw racquets over fences anymore.

Bud Collins

International Tennis Hall of Famer,
Sportscaster and Writer (Boston Globe)

Having played but one set of tennis in my life, being a golfer and having had lunch with TV Producer Gary Smith, who said something to the effect that "Tennis is so much better for you physically," I agreed that it had to be more of a "workout." However, I also foolishly stated that tennis could not be that difficult a sport.

You see, I had always been somewhat of a jock as a young man and just imagined that tennis couldn't be that tough to conquer. In about ten minutes, I hit three balls over the clubhouse into the Beverly Hills Hotel's swimming pool, and they surprised a few water-winged children. Needless to say, had they been closer, I would have apologized. Good manners, as we all know, are a plus to any sport.

I cannot condone what has of late been transpiring on our baseball fields, basketball courts and even in our ice hockey arenas.

These moments of abuse, however, have forever been with us. To try to curtail the aggressiveness of our highly "testosteroned" younger athletes would be one herculean effort. However, let us try to, at least, when it comes to all the Little League fathers.

Robert Goulet
Singer, Actor and Stage Performer

A player must keep in mind that tennis is just a game for most of us. While winning is so important as a reward for all of the long hours of practice, it is not the ultimate goal. The ultimate goal should be to have fun. Etiquette is a crucial part of any sport.

The best example I have is my wife, Wanda. She had been playing for about six months and was hitting the ball extremely well, but had never played a match. When she was pushed into playing a set with someone she did not know, she got embarrassed at 0-4 and wanted to quit. I convinced her that it wasn't proper etiquette.

After practicing and practicing for another six months, she played someone who had beaten her consistently. This time, Wanda beat her opponent 6-0 in the first set and was up 4-0 in the second. It was only after her opponent had literally walked off the court and quit that Wanda understood what I meant. She was not allowed the victory that she had worked so hard for. The fun of the match was gone.

That's why I think etiquette is crucial.

Kenny Rogers
Singer and Songwriter

This is a good guide to tennis etiquette and court manners. I personally prefer wearing "whites" on the court. It looks so crisp and clean. Wimbledon is certainly right in that respect!

Dina Merrill
Actress

When I learn to read, Nancy's book will be the first one I will read. Right now, I am too busy playing tennis to advance my reading lessons. Remember, as in reading or tennis, *i* before *e*, except after *c*.

Tim Conway
Comedian and Actor

Learning the mechanics of our chosen craft, be it dancing, tennis or another, is the first thing we do. Just as important is to learn and, therefore, show respect for the art of each craft and its history.

Nancy Koran has done a wonderful job and a brilliant service to tennis by illuminating every aspect of the game's long-standing etiquette rules, which are so integral to its beauty and grace. Bravo!

Ann Reinking
Choreographer, Dancer and Actress

I thoroughly enjoyed Nancy Koran's book on tennis etiquette. It showed me just how uncouth I really am.

John Sterling
Radio Sports Announcer

The absurd ideal of winning-at-any-cost already has produced so many destructive effects on both our society and culture that you would think we hardly require another lecture on the point. It is competition for high ratings, for example, that is largely responsible for this mostly pitiable state of modern television. The same thing goes for the state of the pop music market.

Not very many years ago, it would have seemed unnecessary to have to defend fairness, honesty and good manners. At present the necessity for such instruction is painfully apparent.

Nancy Koran is delivering the right message at the right time.

Steve Allen

Comedian, Talk Show Host, Actor and Songwriter

Nancy's words have a wider implication and meaning than appear at first glance. Apply them to life, not just the tennis court, and they will work for you.

Adam West

Movie and Television Actor

There's a lot to be learned from athletics. Live by the rules of the game and by the rules of society; otherwise you don't have a good game and you don't have a good society.

Jesse Owens
Olympic Gold Medalist

Foreword

It has been my good fortune to play the game of tennis well enough to compete on the professional circuit, battling it out with many tennis greats—from Rosewall and Laver to Connors, Newcombe, Borg and Smith. I was additionally fortunate to have entered the game during the beginnings of pro tennis. In other words, I have spent many years playing the game for the love of the game.

Tennis, the gentleman's game, which first started as a court game, had decorum and courtesy as part and parcel of the sport. Treating our opponents, umpires, ball kids and fans with respect was something to be expected and to be done willingly. This level of correctness, or etiquette, if you will, gave the players even more in return than it cost us. We enjoyed ourselves!

In *The Zen of Tennis—A Winning Way of Life*, Nancy has written an entertaining, informative book that recalls the strong traditions of tennis sportsmanship. Her book reminds us that we can compete fiercely and still "be nice" and that tennis is a great game of finesse and skill for people of all ages and levels.

Well done, Nancy. We can all benefit from brushing up on the etiquette that makes the game of tennis so unique!

Colin S. Dibley

Introduction

The worn-out expressions "I didn't know" and "I forgot" are really an excuse for poor manners in all human endeavors, whether in social settings, politics or sports.

Of course, tennis has rules and regulations pertaining to the court, equipment and scoring. Yet, respectable court behavior has often been left to the good judgment and common sense of participants, players and spectators. Doing the right thing in tennis and in life, however, may not always be easy or self-evident. Even experienced players sometimes ignore or can forget how to properly comport themselves on and off the court. Recently, as a teaching tennis professional, I have been concerned about the relaxation of civility and good judgment on the tennis court and in the "tennis world." I feel that through the concept of Zen, we can understand the true gifts that tennis has to offer.

Zen, as defined by the Webster's New World Dictionary, is: "Enlightenment that is sought through introspection and intuition." Plato once said, "The life which is unexamined is not worth living."

Playing tennis with Zen is not about how well we play, or how well we understand the theory of tennis. It is more than external conditions. It is a mental attitude that focuses on how we treat and respect the game. If we possess a love for what we are doing, we possess everything. When our own needs are fulfilled, this is mirrored to others who then also reap the benefit of it. This will be true, however, only to the extent that we implement and practice the wisdom of *The Zen of Tennis*.

Nancy Koran

A Note to the Reader

The photographs at the beginning of each chapter are of friends and clients.

Throughout this text, I have used certain titles or words that are basically the same in meaning.

The tennis professional may be referred to as:

Pro

Instructor

Coach

Teacher

Trainer

The student may be referred to as:

Player

Client

Pupil

Learner

Patron

Tennis etiquette may be referred to as:

Proper upbringing

Class

Culture

Sophistication

Pizzazz

Now, the ball's in my court! Are you ready?

Top photo:
Bill Tilden and Rene Lacoste

Bottom photo:
Arthur Ashe

Three Champions known for
their style and grace.

CHAPTER ONE

The History of Tennis

Top photo:
*Hazel Hotchkiss Wightman
(left) and Sarah Palfrey*

*Bottom photo:
Gottfried von Cramm
(right) with Davis Cup
teammate*

Paragons of etiquette.

The History of Tennis

Philosophers agree that to understand the present and properly shape the future we must first study the past. As in life, so it is in tennis necessary for us to maintain our fundamental values. By knowing the history of tennis, it becomes easier to emulate the standard of excellence of past champions, both in play and conduct. Everyone who enjoys the game of tennis today should appreciate the importance of those pioneers who paved the way and breathed life into this tremendous sport with their performance, ability and endless devotion to the game. Basically for the love of it!

The tennis players who contributed to this book were among the greatest not only for their supremacy on the court but for the example they set with their professional behavior. They inspire all players young and old throughout the world. We watch and emulate them for their ability, protocol and goodwill, both on and off the court.

In the Beginning

"Real" or "royal" tennis, as it was called, was played toward the end of the Middle Ages in Europe. It came into being in the thirteenth century in the monastery courtyards of France. It soon became a favorite pastime among royalty who began calling their new sport *Jeu de paume*, meaning "the game of the palm." Real tennis was played indoors in long narrow rooms, which made it challenging to hit the ball through the passages. The court design originated from the monastery cloisters. The method of scoring that we play by today has basically stayed the same (each point being scored by fifteen, such as 15, 30, etc.). The score "forty," which comes after "thirty," is an abbreviation of "forty-five." The word "deuce" (this term denotes that each player has a score of forty) is a derivative of the French word *a deux,* indicating that two points must be won consecutively to win the game.

The word "love" in tennis (having zero points) comes from the French word *oeuf,* which means egg. The oval shape of the egg is symbolic of the numeral "0." The word "serve" comes from the fact that royalty originally had their servants (serve) start the ball to begin each point. Starting the ball seemed a menial task, which is why it was performed by a subordinate. The word racquet is from Latin roots. Initially it was called *reticulum,* meaning small "net." The word later changed to rachetta and then racquet.

During the French revolution tennis almost vanished throughout Europe. After the conflict, tennis began a revival and became even more popular, with tennis clubs built to accommodate its many enthusiasts. It was during the 1870's that a new form of real tennis appeared. It was called "lawn tennis." This new adaptation emerged for many reasons. First, real tennis was played indoors at the monasteries where the courts were not of a uniform size or shape. Second, the upper class (who adopted the sport as their own), found it impractical to travel great distances to play in a cloister. They preferred to entertain their guests at home in their own backyard. Lawn tennis soon became the chosen sport of the upper class. They had the spacious lawns on which to set up a court as well as the financial means for its expensive maintenance. Since tennis was primarily played by the upper class, immense importance was placed on proper etiquette and controlled behavior.

In 1874 Major Walter Wingfield designed and patented his own version of the sport and made it portable so that people could carry all the equipment: net, ball and racquet, along with an instruction booklet. Major Wingfield called his version of the sport *Sphairistike* (Greek word meaning "ball game"). Later the name changed to "Sticky" and then to its more descriptive name, "Lawn Tennis." Soon manufacturers began producing their own portable tennis sets.

In 1877 the England Croquet Club was facing financial ruin. To ameliorate its financial situation it added lawn tennis and changed its name to the All England Croquet and Lawn Tennis Club. New members were invited to compete in a lawn tennis tournament in which the winner would receive a silver cup. This was the start of the Wimbledon championship we know and love today. Initially all rules in regard to equipment, net size, scoring, court dimension, etc. were a bit nebulous, but they were soon to be rewritten.

Tennis Becomes International

Mary Ewing Outerbridge of Staten Island is credited with introducing tennis to the United States in 1874. She discovered the sport while visiting her brother in Bermuda. The equipment was so foreign that it was held up in U.S. Customs for weeks.

The United States National Lawn Tennis Association was established in 1881. It was in this same year that the first official U.S. tennis championship for men was played at the Newport Casino in Rhode Island. The championship was held annually in Newport until 1915 when it was moved to the West Side Tennis Club in Forest Hills, N.Y. (which began as a men's club). In 1924 the Forest Hills site was enlarged to include a tennis stadium — the only one in the country. The U.S. Championship remained there until 1977 and was then relocated to its present site, the National Tennis Center in Flushing, N.Y. In 1887 the USLTA Women's Championship began in Philadelphia at the Philadelphia Cricket Club. It was then moved to Forest Hills and finally to the National Tennis Center in Flushing, N.Y.

In the 1880's it was decided that women should wear white so that their perspiration would not be visible. Before the First World War the overhead service was not used by women due to their restrictive clothing. Proper attire required women to wear long skirts, petticoats, stockings and cumbersome hats. However, as women's tennis became more vigorous, sleeve lengths and hemlines got shorter. In 1919 Suzanne Lenglen, a champion tennis player from France, revolutionized fashion, both on the court and off, with her one-piece, sleeveless dress with a plunging neckline, a hem that extended just below her knee and with stockings rolled just above the knee. At first people were skeptical of Miss Lenglen's style, but soon her dress was copied and became the precedent for, the culotte skirt and the fashions we see today.

In 1900 Davis Cup originated. Unlike Wimbledon and the U.S. Championship, which were reserved for amateurs, Davis Cup was for professionals. In the beginning Davis Cup was a competition between the United States and England but within time extended to any country that had a Lawn Tennis Association. Davis Cup is still played today and is a worldwide competition among more than 50 countries. In 1923 the Wightman Cup (the counterpart of Davis Cup) began as a competition between the ladies of the United States and Great Britain. In 1990, due to the fact that the United States was dominating the event year after year, it was agreed to by both countries to temporarily halt the competition. It has not resumed.

Initially amateur and professional tournaments were separate. The big tournaments were only for amateurs who played for room, board and other expenses. Tennis players who turned professional, however, received little money for playing Davis Cup and traveling the world playing a series of exhibition matches. Before long the rewards of the professional game didn't compare to the lavish gifts, expense payments and perquisites received by amateur players.

Soon tennis's popularity was declining among both amateurs

and professionals. Finally, in 1968 the British Lawn Tennis Association opened Wimbledon to professionals; both amateurs and professionals were allowed to compete together. Soon the other grand slam tournaments would follow. This was the start of the "Open Era." It was a new beginning and talent was unlimited. Along with better players came large crowds, television coverage and big money.

Tennis Today

Twenty-first century tennis is about tiebreakers, 120 mph serves and hundreds of thousands of dollars to the players who win the tournaments. There is no doubt that tennis has evolved, but some people worry that the sport has lost its grace. Not only have the powerful racquets replaced craftiness and finesse with speed and physical power, but the players themselves have changed. Instead of sportsmanship and courtesy there are temper tantrums directed to opponents, umpires, linesmen and the public. Throughout the years tennis has grown because of its idealism. Playing tennis developed individuals not only to be better tennis players but also better people. What we can learn from the history of tennis and past champions, both as athletes and as individuals, is to never abandon pride and dignity. For regardless of score, it is important that we retain our graciousness in our wins as well as our defeats and that we acknowledge our opponents for trying their best. Most importantly, we want to walk off the court and feel proud that we played fair and gave our best effort that day.

Coaches believe the major element of winning in tennis is a strong serve-and-return game. So it is with the Zen of Tennis. What you "serve" to your opponent on and off the court is what he or she will return to you. Similarly, how you and I "serve" the sport of tennis (or others) will affect how that sport (or others) will return many years of future enjoyment to us. Call it Karma, "What comes around goes around," or call it common sense, "What you sow is what you reap."

Sir Winston Churchill once said, "How little we should worry about anything except doing our best." This attitude throughout history has won wars, made leaders great and other people successful and even developed tennis players into true champions. Now you have the scope of this book.

Top: Bjorn Borg

Bottom: Monica Seles

Modern legends whose names are synonymous with class and good sportsmanship.

TENNIS GREATS
SPEAK OUT

John Newcombe

International Tennis Hall of Famer. Ranked number one in the world three years. Winner of many singles and doubles titles, including Wimbledon (singles 3X and doubles 6X), the U.S. Open (singles 2X, doubles 3X and mixed doubles), the French Open (doubles 3X) and the Australian Open (singles 2X, doubles 5X).

What makes a sport great is the history of that sport. Tennis etiquette is an integral part of tennis history.

Margaret Osborne duPont

International Tennis Hall of Famer. Ranked number one in the world four years in a row. Winner of many singles and doubles titles, including Wimbledon (singles, doubles 5X and mixed doubles), the U.S. Open (singles 3X, doubles 13X and mixed doubles 9X) and the French Open (singles 2X and doubles 3X).

Tennis etiquette is so important because it makes for a more enjoyable game. Tennis should be fun. Good etiquette is a result of and a reflection of a person's background and personality. I think everyone wishes to be thought of favorably.

Sportsmanship and good etiquette are such important factors on the tennis court, where lifetime friendships can be won or lost.

Jan Kodes

International Tennis Hall of Famer. Winner of many singles and doubles titles, including Wimbledon (singles) and the French Open (singles 2X). Finished in the world's top ten in singles two years.

Tennis etiquette is one of the most important elements of the sport of tennis and should be well respected. Recently, tennis etiquette seems to be a thing of the past and needs to be restored to the sport. We must realize that many people do watch tennis through television coverage. Poor etiquette is damaging the popularity of tennis.

It is essential that everyone involved in the game, including parents, players, coaches, managers and promoters, try to realize that the lack of tennis etiquette could cost us the very future of our game.

Frew McMillan

International Tennis Hall of Famer. Winner of many singles and doubles titles, including Wimbledon (doubles 3X and mixed doubles 2X), the U.S. Open (doubles and mixed doubles 2X), and the French Open (doubles and mixed doubles). South African Davis Cup player.

Etiquette is respect for the past and the future, respect for the opponent, the officials and the spectators. When you show tennis etiquette, it is only then that you can begin to assume self-respect.

It is comparatively easy to play according to the rules just like a motorist driving in a lane and following the signals. Etiquette is playing in the guidelines and following a true path law-abidingly and in a courteous manner.

Steven Glickstein and Berner Paul,
Delray Beach, Fla.

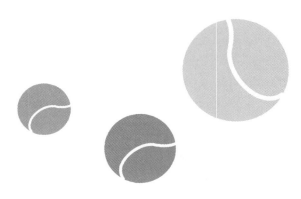

CHAPTER TWO

Sporting Behavior at the Club

Sporting Behavior at the Club

It may seem obvious, but etiquette at the club is just as important as etiquette on the tennis court. The two go hand in hand.

The following alphabetical list of dos and don'ts is based on common sense and will help you to avoid any dirty looks. Take note of the behaviors most people find annoying so that you can avoid them, as well as the guidelines to follow that will enhance both your game and your life.

Alcoholic Beverages: Drinking alcoholic beverages in moderation is acceptable, but you are still responsible for yourself and your actions. What might seem to be fun and playful to you could seem obnoxious to someone else. If you want to "party" at the club, do it after your match and away from serious players.

● ● ●

Courtesy: Be courteous to people behind you by holding the doors for them—holding the doors "open," that is.

However, try not to hold things such as tables, chairs or a court for other people. "First come, first served" is the way things work at most tennis clubs.

No, your racquet leaning against the net is not proper notification that the court is being held for someone else. "Please," "Thank you," and "Excuse me" are words that will also win you big smiles on and off the court, especially after you have interrupted someone's game more than ten times with your errant ball.

When getting a towel or water for yourself, do the same for your partner. Yes, even for your opponent.

Court Reservations: When calling to schedule court time, know the day and time that you wish to play ("one hour for singles, two hours for doubles" is the norm). Always check with the front desk before playing to confirm which court has been reserved for you.

● ● ●

Discretion: Do not get crazy in co-ed Jacuzzis, saunas or steam rooms. Be respectful of others; do your "hanky-panky" off the club premises. Things can and do get out of hand at some clubs.

● ● ●

First Aid: Immediately call the locker room attendant or the front desk if you see someone get hurt or take ill. By the way, do not be so quick to ask if you can use his or her court time.

● ● ●

Gambling: There is no place at all for monetary gambling in tennis because it defeats the essence of the sport. Most people play tennis in order to sharpen their skills of timing, strength and concentration. Depending on one's effort and intent, tennis provides exercise and competition. Most beneficially, the sport offers fun and enjoyment.

As is evident in professional competition, monetary rewards can destroy the "play to have fun" spirit. Small non-monetary wagers, however, are okay. I have encountered players who make it a point to agree ahead of time that the loser will buy refreshments afterward. If both players bring a new can of balls to the match, they can agree that the winner will keep the unopened can and that the loser can take home the used balls from the match.

● ● ●

Gossip: Gossip travels fast. Avoid being a part of it. You are bigger than that, even if you lose 0-6 and 0-6.

Interpersonal Communication: If someone whom you do not recognize acts like your long-lost cousin, reintroduce yourself. You will feel better in the long run. When a person you do not especially like says "Hello," at least try to be courteous and return the greeting. When someone becomes pushy or makes unwanted advances firmly state that you are not "interested" and then leave the area as quickly as possible. If you ever feel you are in danger, seek out immediate help from another club member or staff person.

● ● ●

Lost and Found: If you find something, always turn it in to the lost-and-found desk—even if it is something you need or want. This includes new tennis balls, which may look exactly like the ones you use but forgot to bring.

If you lose something, do check the club's lost-and-found before you accuse anyone. Even if someone has an item that looks exactly like yours, never assume it is yours. There is the story about a man who left his dentures in the locker room....

● ● ●

The Mirror: Do not "hog" the mirror even if you got there first, unless you are 4' 6" tall and the person behind you is 6' 4".

● ● ●

Nail Polish: Keep in mind that a tennis club is not a nail salon. As you know, nail polish can be smelly and messy, as well as impossible to wash out of the towels.

● ● ●

Neatness: Do not clutter space with your belongings. The club is not your private arena, but is to be shared amicably with everyone.

Be clean and show respect to others by picking up after yourself. After you have used a towel or other items, dispose of them properly.

● ● ●

No Smoking Areas: Observe "no smoking" signs. If you are in a group, ask if anyone minds that you smoke. Refrain, if people prefer that you do not. Obviously, be careful as you blow smoke and always extinguish cigarettes in the proper place.

● ● ●

Privacy: Do not take it personally when people are alone and prefer not to be bothered. Do you recall the stranger who sat next to you on the airplane and never stopped talking? Everyone needs his or her space and at times prefers to be left alone. A smile and a "good morning" will be much better received than "Need help with your backhand, buddy?" Also, do not stare when someone is weighing him- or herself or changing clothes. Always respect other people's privacy. One club, I understand, has installed the scale in the bathroom stall for privacy.

● ● ●

Publications: Do not clip or tear out pages from, let alone keep, magazines and newspapers that are provided by the club.

● ● ●

Respect: Everyone deserves equal respect no matter who or what the situation may be; this includes the club staff and attendants. Those who give respect are most likely to be respected back.

● ● ●

Souvenirs: Avoid collecting new "home furnishings" from the club— i.e., towels, combs and ashtrays. This is not only stealing, but

it is tacky. Saying it is "a souvenir of Wimbledon" or "from the club I played at in Nigeria" is a poor excuse.

● ● ●

Tennis Balls: Used tennis balls in the junior practice box are not simply for anyone's taking or convenience. Please buy your own balls.

● ● ●

Waiting: If you are waiting for someone, wait in the lobby by the front desk. You can save time if you let the receptionist know for whom you are waiting and at what time he or she is expected.

● ● ●

Singing in the Locker Room: You may fancy yourself a Pavarotti in the shower, but others may be inclined to disagree. Always be considerate of others. In this situation, take to heart the French expression *fermez la bouche* and do try to "keep your mouth shut."

TENNIS GREATS SPEAK OUT

Pauline Betz Addie

International Tennis Hall of Famer. Formerly ranked number one in the world. Winner of many singles and doubles titles, including Wimbledon (singles), the U.S. Open (singles 4X) and the French Open (mixed doubles).

Etiquette? Thank God we have it. Without it, we might murder our opponent after her skillful backhand passing shot, instead of cheerfully calling out, "Well done!"

Beneath its civilized veneer, tennis is a kind of war. You've got to have that "killer instinct" to be a winner. But you can behave gracefully, like a Stan Smith, rather than follow the entertaining but self-serving antics of a John McEnroe.

Doris Hart

International Tennis Hall of Famer. Winner of many singles and doubles titles, including Wimbledon (singles, doubles 4X and mixed doubles 5X), the U.S. Open (singles 2X, doubles 4X and mixed doubles 5X), the French Open (singles 2X, doubles 5X and mixed doubles 3X) and the Australian Open (singles, doubles and mixed doubles 2X). Achieved the "hat trick" in 1954 at the U.S. Open, winning all events (singles, doubles and mixed doubles).

Tennis etiquette is nothing more than good sportsmanship. The two go hand in hand.

Vic Seixas

International Tennis Hall of Famer. Winner of many singles and doubles titles, including Wimbledon (singles and mixed doubles 4X), the U.S. Open (singles, doubles 2X and mixed doubles 3X), the French Open (doubles 2X and mixed doubles) and the Australian Open (doubles). Finished in the world's top ten in singles eight years.

Etiquette has been defined as "the conduct or procedure required by good breeding or prescribed by authority in social or official life." In tennis, the "Rules of the Game" are the authority. In order to get the most enjoyment from our sport, one needs to observe the rules and conduct oneself in a way that shows good breeding.

The way we act on the court is a good indication of how we meet the challenges of life off the court. While there have been others, Chris Evert and Stan Smith are two players who exemplified proper tennis etiquette throughout their careers. They have been champions both on and off the court.

Gladys M. Heldman

International Tennis Hall of Famer. Founder of the Virginia Slims and the Avon Futures Circuit. Founder and publisher of World Tennis Magazine. Winner of the National Service Bowl awarded to women who have made the most outstanding contribution to tennis.

In Japan, some tennis resorts have as many as 250 courts. When all the courts are filled, you never hear players shouting or banging racquets on the court or arguing about calls. All you hear is the "pock, pock, pock" of balls being hit. When a match is over and you have won, the opponents will say, "You were too good." If they have won, they'll say, "Next time you'll win."

If you hit a lob-volley short, no one will smack a ball in your face. If you have an off day and think you have ruined the match, your partner and your opponents will cheer you up. The fine points of tennis etiquette predominate, and that is the reason why playing tennis in Japan is so much fun.

Cassandra Fox, New York, N.Y.

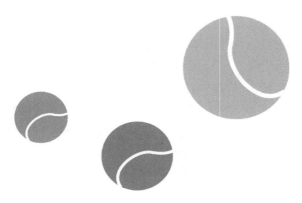

CHAPTER THREE

What's Cricket and What's Not

What's Cricket and What's Not

Let us now discuss the meaning of "cricket" behavior, both on and off the tennis court. Because I began playing tennis at a relatively young age, I have benefited tremendously by watching and imitating others. Playing often at private clubs and public courts and also being a keen observer, I became conditioned to the expectations of tennis etiquette.

What, where, when and how to do and not to do certain things on and off the court constitute what is known as "The Code." This system consists of rules relating to tennis behavior and play that we are expected to know.

Even though so much of tennis etiquette is simply common sense, etiquette can easily be forgotten, avoided and taken for granted. Occasional slip-ups can thus occur at all levels of the sport, which, in turn, can lead to behavior that is unbecoming, even unethical, on and near the court. Such behavior, which includes racquet-throwing, spitting and verbal profanities, or what disciplinarians may often refer to as "not sport" or "not cricket," reflects a serious lack of tennis etiquette.

We easily recognize this type of behavior in others because we view the action from afar when we are relaxed and calm and have clear judgment. However, if we are directly involved in the action, it is easy to become overly excited and lose our perspective.

You can learn about this behavior in several ways. First, take time to observe the attitudes and behavior of other participants at tournaments, your club or at public courts. Second, learn and put into actual practice the proper attitude and behavior of tennis etiquette.

The key is putting into practice what you know and being an

example for others. Once you master the rules of proper tennis etiquette, I can assure you that they will become part of your winning style.

The saying "practice makes perfect" holds true for tennis strokes, and for learning to control our mental attitude and to do relaxation techniques. Try to always remain calm, cool and aware of the warning signs leading to aggravation, the silent bombshell that results in improper behavior and unnecessary embarrassment.

The etiquette questions for this chapter have been divided into four time frames: (1) before you get on the court, (2) when you are ready to begin your match, (3) while you are playing the match, and (4) after you have played your match.

Before You Play

At a social match, I overheard a player suggest that since his opponent had brought sunglasses and a sun visor, he should play the entire match on the sunny side of the court. It sounds as if he is really trying to bend the rules. Is this common?

Be careful. If you agree to that change, your opponents might next suggest that you hit balls only to their forehand. In a short time, they might tell you about the Brooklyn Bridge and describe the good deal you could get it for.

Elsewhere in this book, I talk about the importance of keeping your tennis bag stocked with all your playing equipment. Sunglasses and a sun visor are part of that equipment. If you neglect to bring them, that is really your problem, as the forgetful player, to solve. Changing sides, as stated in the rules, is the proper procedure.

The rules of tennis were established to equalize the sport for the participants. They also help to avoid conflict and argumentation.

Deviation is unfair to both the sport and the players.

During a lesson, the instructor may insist that he or she should remain on the sunny side so that the sun will not interfere with the student's practice session.

● ● ●

By practicing tennis etiquette, will I actually play better tennis?

Definitely! Practicing tennis etiquette stimulates fun and enjoyment in the game and develops an enthusiasm to play and practice. That, of course, means that your game gets better. Successful individuals, including athletes, will tell you that they attribute success to loving and enjoying what they do. This is just what the protocols of tennis etiquette should do for you.

● ● ●

I'm a novice. So, am I expected to know the rules of tennis?

One does not begin to drive a car without knowing the rules of the road. So, what makes you think you could learn to play tennis without knowing the rules?

A novice plays to have fun and to improve at the game. In order to accomplish either goal, it is important for you to learn the rules and "The Code." Memorizing all the rules at the beginning is not necessary, but do learn the basics and how to keep score.

● ● ●

I have played tennis all my life. I've gotten this far without knowing what you call "The Code," so why should I bother now?

It is important to come to the court physically prepared with proper attire, new tennis balls and two racquets (in case a string should break). In the same way, it is also important to be mentally prepared by knowing both the rules of the game and correct tennis etiquette. Physical as well as mental preparation will help you to experience more fun and fulfillment as you play and give you a much greater appreciation for the game.

● ● ●

I am totally confused. After taking tennis lessons for years and practicing at a maniac's pace, I don't feel I have progressed very far in my game. What am I doing wrong, and what can I do to get better results from my efforts?

So many people play tennis, each with different habits and abilities, that it would be impossible to conclude that after having had "X" number of lessons and "Y" amount of practice time, all players should progress at the same rate.

Keep in mind that the variety of strokes, spins, court surfaces and strategies makes tennis a challenging and interesting sport.

One thing is certain: With lessons and practice, an individual is bound to be better than someone without lessons and practice.

So, these are my recommendations:

- If the pressure to excel is hampering your play, practice relaxing and having fun in your game.

- If your lessons do not seem to be helping, try a different coach whom you feel understands your game and goals.

- If your practice pace becomes frantic, practice less and try to allow more time for actual game play.

- Work on your strengths and weaknesses. Match play is not the best time to experiment with a new stroke, technique or strategy. Stick to what is familiar and comfortable.

- If some opponents are consistently beating you on the

court, analyze their game when you are playing them or when they are playing others. Find out what their weaknesses are and try to play to those weaknesses.

- Play against weaker players to help perfect your strokes and strategy and build up your confidence—an important ingredient of winning. This will make a difference when you play others. Keeping a ball in play against a weak player can be quite a challenge in itself, since it teaches patience and consistency, two essential traits in mastering tennis and life.

Never give up the game and never lose sight of the importance of having fun in playing your sport. Learning tennis is a fun but slow process, but with patience it can be very rewarding.

● ● ●

The rules of tennis seem to be the same throughout the world. Except for languages and types of court surfaces, are there any other differences from country to country? How can tennis etiquette be the same worldwide?

One of the greatest things about tennis is that nationality, age, sex, race, religion and politics are not relevant to the game. The rules of the game and basic etiquette are universal. Of course, there are eccentrics who take liberties with the rules of play and etiquette and even make up their own rules, such as calling a "let" (a take-over) when they miss a return, claiming they were not ready, or saying, "I'll be playing with this new racquet, which is 30 inches round and 60 inches long." Thank goodness this is more extreme behavior rather than the norm.

● ● ●

If friends invite me to play tennis at their private club, am I

expected to pay the guest fee?

As a guest, it is proper to offer to pay the guest fee or the court fee or to split the cost down the middle. Naturally, the offer will be appreciated, but seldom will the host or the hostess accept the offer. It would be a nice gesture to invite your friend for lunch or drinks outside the club. If you belong to a private club, extend your host an invitation. Otherwise, a social dinner out will suffice nicely.

A thank-you note is another sign of good etiquette. Even if you are a tremendous player with many offers to play, never become so egotistical you become a leech, always looking for the free game.

● ● ●

When I am invited to play at a private club, should I expect to be able to use the locker room and shower facilities?

Normally, yes. The member who has invited you should include all the comforts of the club facilities in the invitation, even if you end up enjoying them on your own. He or she is expected to direct you regarding where to go and introduce you to staff and friends, who will be more than happy to assist you.

● ● ●

Are there still some clubs that do not allow or feel uncomfortable with players of certain races or religions?

There certainly are. Fortunately, they are becoming fewer in number each year. While token representation sometimes still exists in the areas of race, religion and age, much progress has been made in the right direction. The Zen of Tennis philosophy is about respecting all players regardless of their race, religion, sex or sexual preference without any reservation whatsoever.

● ● ●

At public courts, I find it annoying that people are not aware

of the procedure for proper court succession. Is this feeling justified?

Most novice players do not know all the procedures and rules for play at public courts and clubs; this can be quite frustrating for both parties (those who know and those who don't).

Why not turn an annoyance into a pleasantry? If you see new-comers approach wearing an uncertain look on their faces, point out that there is a sign-up sheet or mention, "I guess that you will be having the court after us." I strongly suggest you never let yourself get uptight or upset before going out on the court. Stress will adversely affect your concentration and enjoyment of the game.

● ● ●

It has been an overcast day with misty rain off and on and the threat of more to come. Should I assume that my match has been canceled and call to verify this, or should I just take the chance that the courts are actually playable?

Always call! While it may be raining against my windows, the weather might be clear three blocks away. Likewise, depending on the court surface, an early rain may have little or no effect on court play.

Occasionally in inclement weather, the players will play inside if indoor courts are available. Most importantly, call the club in advance, since it shows that you respect the other players in your group—always a sign of good etiquette!

● ● ●

Often I find players badly mismatched, simply because they had no idea (or they lied) about their true playing level. Is there a standard rating system for a person's level of play? How can it be maintained so that everyone enjoys the game?

The United States Tennis Association (USTA) has formulated the

standard rating system called the National Tennis Rating Program (NTRP). This system rates players from 1.0 (a player just starting to play tennis) to level 7.0 (a world-class player), with one-half (.5) increment levels between these numbers. Most players fall between 3.0 and 5.0. Sanctioned personnel provide the rating at many clubs at pre-arranged times and places. Most local tennis clubs can provide you with supplemental information and phone numbers.

Once an NTRP rating has been obtained, players find it best to play at their level in order to enjoy the game. I find occasionally playing one level higher can also add incentive, offering a good opportunity for players to improve. Usually, tournaments are organized based on the NTRP rating levels. You would not be allowed to compete at a level below your rating, for obvious reasons.

● ● ●

Who's responsible for bringing the tennis balls to a match? Is it acceptable to use balls from a previous match?

Every player should keep a new can of balls in his or her tennis bag at all times. When you are invited to play a match, usually the person setting up the match breaks open his or her new can, even if the guest insists otherwise. In the rare situation that neither player has a new can of balls, make a big apology before playing with the balls previously used.

● ● ●

Even if I am of the same NTRP level and have a good disposition, is it possible that other players at times may refuse to play with me? Is there a reasonable solution?

In social tennis, people do have the prerogative to play with whomever they wish. However, in tournaments, players cannot choose, since they play according to the draw schedule. Private clubs may have a players' ladder, whereby you have the right to challenge the next two or three players above yourself. Another good suggestion is to play with people who enjoy your company and your game, so that you will not lose the fun and relaxation factor in tennis.

● ● ●

There are several players at my club whom I would enjoy meeting and playing tennis with. I could walk up and introduce myself, but I am afraid of hearing the response "We'll have to play sometime, but I'm so busy now I don't know when I'll be free." Is there a better approach?

Try to have a mutual friend or the club pro introduce you. Go up to the player off the court or outside the locker room. It is more likely that he or she will be comfortable, relaxed and more receptive. After exchanging names, say something such as "I've seen you play, and your style of game is one I'd like to play against. I have some court time this afternoon. Would you like to join me?"

Even if you get a rejection, try to keep the conversation on tennis (which you both have in common): "Where did you learn your game? Ever go to a tennis camp? Under which pro or pros have you studied?" Try to avoid more personal questions such as "Where do you live? Married? What type of work do you do?" and so on. You could conclude with "Could I interest you in a refreshment?"

● ● ●

Players who bring cellular phones onto a tennis court really irk me. Hearing the ring or seeing them talk on the phone is a distraction to everyone within earshot. How many emergencies could there be that cannot wait until court time is over?

I suggest that cellular phones be turned off when carried onto the tennis court. Leave the number of the tennis club with family and friends. An interruption should be left solely for an emergency. Usually the attendant at the front desk will notify you when an emergency occurs.

Exhibitionists who must show off their importance probably want the attendant to announce all their personal calls over the public address system, including how the Tokyo stock market closed and if their racehorse won today! On court, I have noticed that cellular phone users have a difficult time retaining playing partners.

● ● ●

I have been matched up to play someone new in the club. Instead of enjoying the exercise and the new competition, my opponent interrogates me as if I am under suspicion and he works for the C.I.A. Is a personal dossier necessary before we walk onto the court?

Definitely not! Exchange names and limit the balance of your conversation to questions about tennis. Try to avoid getting personal and delving into your opinions of other players. If the relationship seems to be worth exploring, continue your conversation off the court or over some bit of refreshment. On the court, it is important to feel comfortable and enjoy your game.

● ● ●

When someone says, "Let's play sometime" or "I will give you a call soon," I immediately get turned off. Experience has taught me that these are the most insincere expressions in a tennis player's repertoire. How do I know when an invitation is sincere?

You will know only when you take advantage of the other person's invitation. When I hear similar comments, my response is: "Let's set up something right now. I have this day and time available. So, can you make it?" If they hem and haw, I move on to other players.

Try not to take it personally. While many players will act con-

genial, they sometimes fail to mean what they say. I keep my tennis appointment pad in my racquet bag at all times and religiously note every appointment and opportunity, since I find it a pleasure to play and always look forward to my next match.

● ● ●

My practice partner is perpetually late. Since he evidently thinks that I am not important enough for him to be prompt, I feel that he is being personally disrespectful. Do you agree?

I agree completely. It is inconsiderate and disrespectful when people are chronically late. As unfortunate as his behavior is for you, I also have a little sympathy for him, knowing that he will not be playing tennis for very long.

If a player makes a habit of coming late, he or she will not have sufficient time to stretch and condition him- or herself before playing. Sooner or later, injury is bound to happen.

Needless to say, emergencies can disrupt well-laid plans. With a simple telephone call, you can reschedule the time or locate another partner. Of course, you can claim that the play time is a half-hour earlier than it really is; this sometimes does more harm than good, throwing everyone off schedule.

Unfortunately, this will probably not work with the chronically tardy player either. Thus, it is best to confront the situation head-on. You can give your partner a wristwatch with the ultimatum: come on time ready to play or find a new partner.

● ● ●

Are alcoholic beverages ever permitted on a tennis court?

No! Besides slowing your responses, they can blur your vision. The chances of tripping over your slowly responding feet, running into the net or the posts, or even getting hit by an errant racquet swing are real, as well as dangerous, possibilities. In addition, permitting alcoholic beverages on public courts or on club courts will open up the owners and those responsible to unimaginable liabilities. Booze on the tennis court can lead you to the blues in another "court."

● ● ●

People who bring their children, dogs or radios to tennis courts disturb me. The crying, talking, barking and music can be terribly annoying and extremely distracting. What is your opinion?

Small children (usually in a stroller) should never be brought onto the tennis court. It is a space restricted for players. Those who bring children onto the court do not realize the possibility of injury (stray balls, flying racquets, strollers as obstacles and so on). Children can be placed behind the fencing, where they will be safe. If they are noisy, it is the parent's duty to quiet them or take them home.

Dogs should be tied to the outside fence. If they bark or whine, the owner should quiet them or take them home. Animal waste is also a problem on or around the court. Most private tennis courts will not permit dogs on or near the court.

Unless you are playing on your own court, radios are not permitted. What may seem like music to some may be noise to others.

● ● ●

A stranger approached me and asked if I would hit with him. Since my playing time is limited, I need to be more selective with whom I play. Besides, I know that the individual who is making the request has a lower rating than mine. Is there a way I can refuse his or her invitation gently and gracefully?

First, never be rude or impolite to anyone's request. Second, always thank people for the invitation and then carefully explain that you have a "limited playing time" schedule. Conclude by saying, "If my schedule allows me more free time, I will let you know. Then maybe we can arrange something together."

A few things can happen that may allow you a future opening. The other person may improve his or her play. You may find you have a lot of extra time in your schedule to play. Also, you might discover that the person turns out to be the bank officer who turned down your business loan application. In all seriousness, I recommend reversing the situation in your mind. If Pete Sampras were to come to my club and I asked if he had time to hit with me, what greater thrill would I have than to hear him say, "Great, let's go hit."

In tennis, you will find three types of players: those better than you, those at your same ability level and those not as good as you. It is amazing how people in each category can move up or down at any time—and so can you.

● ● ●

During the warm-up phase of a match, my opponent talks either to me or to other players on the adjacent court. Does the advice of being silent during a match also extend to the warm-up time?

If the talking disturbs you, it also may annoy others. This form of interference is contrary to "The Code." Socializing should be done before you walk onto the court to play or else after the match. Unless it pertains directly to the match, minimize your talking during the warm-up and especially during match play.

● ● ●

Like everyone else, I want to play against those who play a little better than I do. Unfortunately, at my club, they consistently pair me off with players not as good as I am. At first,

I accepted this gracefully, but lately I've been getting annoyed. Any suggestions?

The notion that we play better against players who are better than we are is definitely true. It applies to the players against whom you play and also to the ones who play against you. If we are 3.5 NTRP rated, we often put our names on a list of 3.5 to 4.0 players.

Those who are 3.0 rated often put their names on the same list. After all, it makes them feel better and try harder!

Look at every match as a learning experience. If you continue to beat your opponent with great ease, why not try a different game plan than usual? Why not start executing the new serve and volley that you have recently learned? Experiment and go for low percentage shots, more drop shots and more angles.

It is to your advantage to experience all game styles and levels of play. Explain your situation to whoever is assigning the matches, so they will be able to help line up better competition for you, which you may regret or love.

Beginning Your Match

My opponent wants to warm up forever. How much time should be permitted for warm-ups?

Usually, ten minutes is allotted for a warm-up. If you need more time, do what the pros do and arrange for practice time before the match. Also, be alert to the fact that some tournaments and league matches specify the amount of warm-up time permitted.

● ● ●

In my warm-up before a match, my opponent doesn't return the ball to me. He keeps trying to hit the corners and does whatever he can to keep me from loosening up or, as the term

implies, from warming up. With limited warm-up time, how can I straighten out both him and the tennis ball?

Ask your opponent to come up to the net. Then, explain that the purpose of keeping the ball in play is to allow both of you to hit as many balls as possible in the limited amount of warm-up time.

If this problem occurs often, as an extra precaution consider doing a warm-up with someone else before an important match. And why not? After all, the pros do it. If you follow this advice, you will be ready to play as soon as you step onto the court for your match.

While a warm-up refers to a physical warm-up, it can also serve another purpose—sizing up your opponent. Returning the ball to various areas on the court permits you to observe and analyze your opponent's movement, type of strokes, strengths and weaknesses.

If you spot a flaw, you may want to take it into account in your game plan throughout the match. During your warm-up, you must place the ball where your opponent is able to react to it properly. As you keep the ball in play, study your opponent's style, and do not give away your own secret weapon or game plan.

You can set a good example. Practice control as you keep the ball in play and also be considerate of your opponent. Following this advice, you will find yourself in the favorable position of controlling the ball throughout the points, as well as the match.

● ● ●

We are about to start our match, and my opponent holds only one ball in his hand. The other balls are against the fence. Maybe he feels that if the first serve is not in and he needs a second ball, he can always go over and get a ball. I feel that it delays the game. Should I insist that he have two balls readily available before serving?

Not having two balls available before serving interrupts the continuous play of the game. In my personal experience, there have been times when the second ball was so far away that I felt obligated to tell my opponent to start again: "Take two." This was unfair to me.

There is no reason why a player could not begin serving with the second ball readily available. Explain this to your opponent.

● ● ●

My opponent wants to play as soon as we get on the court without any warm-up. Is this allowable?

You should always extend to your opponent the courtesy of at least ten minutes to warm up, unless both of you agree to a shorter time.

While You Play

Some players seem to act so uptight and serious about a simple practice match. How can I relieve the tension and keep it a fun thing?

Etiquette, like stress and anger, is contagious. I remember one occasion while I was playing in college when one of the players on the other team started complaining about line calls. This complaining then spread like wildfire to every court and every player to the extent that everyone became upset and expressed their anger.

Reverse the situation. When you display etiquette, people tend to follow. As a result, everyone will have a fun time, regardless of who is winning. Before, during and after the match, remain positive and relaxed. With that type of attitude, you will be scheduling your next match with that same partner even before you leave the court.

● ● ●

I have heard that some players win more matches by "psyching out" their opponents than by their strokes. If the player

with the most talent is expected to be the most likely winner, how can we account for such charlatan behavior?

There is a difference between playing smart tennis and "psyching out" an opponent. Smart tennis utilizes several abilities, including being able to stroke better, to outlast your opponent with greater stamina, to create and carry out a better game plan and to outthink your opponent during the match.

"Psyching out" an opponent means trying to intimidate the opponent mentally. You could employ several tricks to "psych out" a player, including scowling at an opponent, muttering harsh words loud enough for the opponent to hear, throwing a temper tantrum every time a shot is missed or repeatedly questioning calls.

This type of behavior is not only futile but results in emotional drainage and distracts both parties—leaving no enjoyment at all. It is likely that you can fool some of the people some of the time, but not all of the people all of the time. This is why "psyching out" your opponent does not win more matches than a good solid game plan. True talent always prevails. However, real talent involves more than great strokes. For this reason, you need to realize how important it is to practice mentally as well as physically.

Keep your mind focused on nothing else but the ball. By ignoring distractions, you keep your opponent, the spectators and all other external conditions from bothering you. When distracted, use deep breaths to relax and focus. Practice playing in this "zone." Try to concentrate on each game, point by point. Focus your attention on the ball, rather than on what is happening around you.

With practice, this technique will help you to reduce feelings of frustration and appreciate the significance of tennis etiquette.

● ● ●

I've encountered opponents who habitually make line calls not only on their side of the court but on mine, too! This often

occurs when I am returning a serve. My opponent, who is serving, will make no attempt to play the ball, stating that the serve was "out." My winning return is not played, making me feel that I've missed an opportunity to win the point. Suitable advice, please?

I "cured" a few people who pulled that trick by moving over to the other service box, while stating, "I'm sorry. I played it as I saw it, and it is my call." Be affirmative.

I suggest that you make all the "out" calls loud and clear to avoid an argument. If necessary, tell the server: "I can see the ball better at 18 feet from the service line than you can see it 60 feet on the other side with a net obstructing your view."

Also, emphasize to your opponent: "You make the calls on your side, and I will make them on my side of the court."

● ● ●

To what extent should I go to distract an opponent, particularly on an overhead or other critical stroke?

I dislike the word distract because it also denotes "to disturb" or "to unsettle." Certainly, foot-stomping, screaming and wildly waving one's arms are out of the question and very unfair. What I do find acceptable and ethical is to watch your opponent's eyes and then make a head or body feint.

You could also extend your arms outward to make it appear that you are covering more of the court. This type of action is not done to distract your opponent. Instead, it is a way of faking your position in the hope that your opponent will return the ball to a place you anticipate on the court.

Talking or laughing when a point is being made is unnecessary and unacceptable. In fact, any noise can be misconstrued for calling a ball "out" or calling a "let."

When hitting a powerful shot, grunting is acceptable unless it is excessively loud. Exaggerated grunting, however, will disturb not only opponents but also those on nearby courts.

● ● ●

What is "no ad" scoring?

"No ad" (or no advantage) scoring will help to expedite play in an unofficial match. The first person to reach a score of four is the winner of the match, in which the scoring is done in numerical sequence (1, 2, 3 and 4). If the players tie at three each, the receiving person or team has the option to indicate from which side (deuce or advantage court) he or she wishes to receive the final served ball. Conducting yourself properly and knowing how to keep score can make the match a more pleasurable experience for you and your opponent.

● ● ●

How should I handle intimidation on the tennis court? The long eye contact, a curled-up lip and that low inner growl make me want to default the match, pack up my gear and go home for the day.

Intimidation usually occurs in tournament play, when most players are more desperate to win. That ploy does seem to be part of some players' game plan. So, if they cannot win due to their own ability, you can be sure they will try the bullying tactic.

(Sad to say, even I have been subjected to vulgarities and threats from people truly needing tennis etiquette.)

My suggestion is simply to try to ignore such a player. Say the least that you can in the process of passing each other on opposite ends of the net when you change sides. Also, try to avoid being in a place where you can hear or see the other player's actions.

Intimidation is a result of low self-esteem both on the court and in life. Win or lose, I would report the player's attitude and tactics to the tournament referee and the other players.

When I feel rushed by my opponent on the court, what can I do?

The simplest way to slow down your opponent is to turn your back before he or she serves or to raise your racquetless hand into the air. Some players keep a towel nearby to dry their hands in an attempt to intentionally slow down play. All of these tactics indicate that you are not ready to begin the next point.

Although tennis play is expected to be without interruption, no player should feel pressured or rushed. Remember that you are entitled to have a full 25 seconds between points; so take advantage of the allotted time. Also, there is no need to rush when retrieving balls and making court changeovers.

You can set the pace by asking your opponent, "Are you ready?" Normally, he or she will reciprocate. If your opponent is ready, he or she will be in the proper place to return serve and in the ready position with eyes up and focused on the server. If you are in doubt, the wisest thing is to ask.

It is also good etiquette at the start of match play for the server to hold up the balls before serving the first point. This type of gesture gives your opponent the clear signal that you have finished all your practice serves and are ready to begin playing points.

Also, as you hold up the ball, you are signaling to everyone that match play is about to commence. It is a good idea to do this whenever new balls are used throughout a match.

● ● ●

Whenever I play against good friends, I find that I'm not competitive and, generally speaking, too nice. Is this what is meant by the term "social tennis"? How can I stimulate my competitiveness?

Tennis would not be half as interesting if it were not for its competitive aspect. If one detaches from the excitement of competition,

you might as well be at a tea party.

During match play, lay aside some of that friendship and look at each other as opponents, with one of you wanting to excel over the other. Several professionals who are very close friends play each other often and never slow down their competitive attitude. After a match, it is hard to tell who the loser is, since they always walk away as friends joking about the next match. I find that refreshing.

If you play by the rules and adhere to tennis etiquette, you will always be nice but never too nice. Years ago when I was playing tennis in the junior ranks, I felt uncomfortable playing my close friend. Because I played passively, my friend, who played to beat me, felt no twinge of discomfort in winning. When I finally reversed the winning record, we still remained best friends.

Maintaining the competitive spirit does justice to you and your game, as well as to your opponent's game. Winning has little merit if an opponent lets up in order for you to win.

● ● ●

After a match, my partner sometimes invites me to have a drink with him. Usually he is dripping with sweat and even smells a bit offensive. What should I do without offending him?

Bring extra towels onto the court so that your partner can dry himself off. Also, you might suggest that you each take a quick shower before you meet each other in the clubhouse for a drink. Explain to your partner that you want to freshen up a bit first.

● ● ●

Does individual behavior on the court have a correlation to behavior off the court?

I find this correlation to be true quite often. Many aggressive, temperamental players on the court also handle their lives and general activities in a similar way. By the same token, many reserved individuals may act relatively quiet and laid-back when they play.

I cannot emphasize enough how essential it is to learn and practice tennis etiquette. In addition to teaching us how to remain calm and to gain control of stressful situations on the court, the discipline will naturally carry over into our everyday lives.

● ● ●

Is it possible to go overboard in motivating yourself while playing?

Yes, you can overdo personal motivation. I suggest that you aim for the middle ground. That light tap on your leg, a slightly visible fist pump and even the hardly audible word of encouragement are always acceptable. However, what makes a player look like the savage conqueror who "crosses the line" is the loud outburst and the "iron fist wave" as if one is smashing an atom. Subtleties of excitement always reflect refinement and good etiquette.

● ● ●

Some people think that if your opponent notices your frustration, it can improve his or her performance. Is this true?

Absolutely! If you lose control of your emotions and concentration, you definitely will not play as well. Your opponent may improve because he or she is playing loose and feels relaxed. You, however, may be worrying about how and why you lost the last point, and all the while your opponent may be planning how to win the next one.

If you get frustrated with your play, first try to slow down. Avoid rushing into the next point or the next serve. You can try rearranging the strings on your racquet to refocus your thoughts. Then take some deep breaths as you think positively that the next point is going to be yours. And more than likely, it will be.

A pro is willing to fight for every point, even the last one of the match, and so should you be.

What can I do when my opponent has the nerve-racking habit of bouncing the ball 20 or 30 times before he or she serves? What do the rules say about this?

The official rules of tennis say nothing about bouncing the tennis ball prior to beginning a serve. As long as there is no delay in the game, you are forced to block it out of your mind and pace yourself accordingly. It might help to consider that such nerve-racking habits often are harmless, even unintentional. After the match you can jokingly ask your opponent, "Did more fuzz come off the balls by bouncing them than by hitting them?"

● ● ●

It really confuses me when my opponent returns every serve, whether it was in or out, and doesn't make the call until the ball is back on my side of the net. I'm chasing the ball over the court before I hear the "out" call. Sometimes, it seems as if the call was made based on my opponent's returned ball. Some players assume that I can tell from my side of the court whether the serve is good and don't say anything. Isn't this unfair to the server?

Very unfair, since it appears to be a doubtful call. As such, the server should get the benefit of the doubt. The rules state that the "out" call should be made instantly. Instead of returning "out" serves over the net, the receiving player should let them go by or hit them to the side of the court or into the net on his or her side. In all cases, a quick call is made. If a player accidentally returns an "out" serve, an apology should follow.

It seems to me only fair that when a player repeatedly returns an "out" serve over the net, he or she should give the server a free repeat serve. Also, keep in mind that the receiver who has disrupted the rhythm of the server is the one who delayed the game.

Why do some players think it is fair to call for a "take-it-over" (to replay the point), when they seem to be in doubt about whether the ball was in or out of the court?

Even one percent of doubt warrants that you give the point to your opponent. When questioned, the one making the call may exclaim, "Well, the ball looked like it was out, and so I gave you the benefit of the doubt." Note the doubt, even hesitation, expressed in that remark. With even the slightest doubt, you should give the point to your opponent. Your response will then be considered fair and "cricket," with no need to replay the point.

● ● ●

Who should keep the score: the server, the receiver or both?

Both players have the responsibility of keeping score. However, the server has the added responsibility of calling out the score loudly enough that the receiver hears it before beginning the next point. It is very easy to forget the score after a long point; so, I recommend that each player keep a mental note of how the points were made, just in case the score is challenged.

● ● ●

Would you explain the proper procedure for retrieving an errant ball going onto an adjacent court? How about the reverse situation of a ball coming onto our court?

I have seen both the worst and the best reactions when a ball rolls onto another court. Some players will pick up the stray ball and hit it wildly in the direction from which it came, without any regard to where it will land. Other players will pretend the ball is not on their court. Still others will pick up the ball and use it in their own game until reminded that the ball is not theirs.

I suggest that you call out a loud "let" the moment you see a ball coming onto the court. Then, pick up the ball and call out in the direction from which it came, "I have a Wilson #4. Whose ball is it?" When the other player says, "Thank you," respond with a courteous "no problem" as you gently hit the ball to the nearest player.

If your ball happens to go into another court, wait until they have finished playing their point. Then, excuse your interruption and gently ask, "Would you mind getting my ball when you have a chance?" If your own ball strays on a court near you but is close enough for you to retrieve it, say "Excuse me" and retrieve it quickly. In all cases, wait inconspicuously until after the next court has completed their point before requesting or retrieving the ball.

● ● ●

Is it possible to be excessively nice on the tennis court?

Yes. I find that players are being too nice when they continually say, "I'm sorry," every time they hit a ball into the net or out of the court. Somehow, they feel that every shot should be perfectly placed and that they are not allowed to make a mistake.

Players are also too nice when they want to give you every point, even those you know were a foot out of the court. They will insist that you take a third serve for no reason at all.

At heart, most players want to win fair and square and with real dignity—that is, by the rules of the game in accordance with tennis etiquette. It is frustrating playing opposite someone who gives you free points and eliminates the sporting challenge to earn them.

● ● ●

My friend is a real gentleman when he plays against other acquaintances and strangers. When he plays against me on the court, he turns into a nasty villain. Tennis manners and fun seem to evaporate when we play together. Is it acceptable to forget tennis etiquette when playing with friends?

Playing against a friend or a foe should not negate proper tennis etiquette, which requires practice for it to become a natural response.

If your friend seems to lack consistency when both of you are playing, bring up the subject in a jovial manner. Say something like the following: "If you're that nasty when you play against me as your friend, I sure would hate to play you as my enemy! So, cool down, buddy, and relax. Let's show that we're friends and are having fun. Now, tell me, what is the secret to beating you easily today?"

● ● ●

What does the comment "She is my best friend off the court, but a perfect stranger or enemy on the court" really mean?

Often among friends, a player's on-the-court behavior can be misconstrued or misunderstood. Perhaps the friend's attitude appears more serious on the court than it does socially off the court. There may be no apology for beating you in straight sets, not even a flinch at hitting a winning shot past or away from you. You will overcome uncomfortable feelings if you don't take it personally. Tennis etiquette requires each player to try to win fairly, even in a friendly game.

Friends should encourage us to be competitive, since it is with our friends that we can learn to face rivalry without anger. I once played with a friend who made a senseless excuse every time I faulted my second serve, saying things such as "Oh, take another serve. I wasn't looking." However, when I had to face real opponents in tournament matches, I expected them to behave just as my friend had done. I learned fast. Without honest competition, you might as well be playing against the practice wall.

● ● ●

When I'm winning a match, I find that practicing tennis etiquette is no problem. However, the minute I find myself los-

ing, my attitude starts to make a complete reversal. Talk about a Jekyll and Hyde! Am I alone in this reaction?

I know exactly how you react, since I see it often in some of the students that I teach. This is one part of the game they do not practice, because the only time they face the problem is when they are losing a match and the pressure is on. The best way to practice being a gracious loser is to concentrate on what I always stress: enjoy the game and have fun while you are making your best effort.

Relax, remain calm and smile, even if you are losing. That may sound dumb but it really works. One girl I taught carried a ragdoll in her tennis bag. Whenever she was losing a match, she would always take out the doll while switching sides of the court, start to talk to it and ask, "Now, how did you say I can beat this girl I'm playing?" That made her and everyone around her smile, except for her opponent, who was too busy listening to the doll!

● ● ●

I hear players shout to their opponents, "Great shot," after they have hit a winner, but is that necessary? I certainly don't want to encourage my opponent's play if my goal is to win the match.

It is a beautiful sight to see professional players applaud their opponents when they have hit a clean winner. That kind of response is a class act. Acknowledging your opponent's great shot is not only courteous, but also shows true respect for his or her ability.

Courtesy returns to those who give it. Your reaction and spontaneous compliment will keep you and your opponent relaxed and will help you to enjoy the match more. Remember, though, praise only the great shots—not everything that comes over the net.

It annoys me when opponents do not say whether the ball I hit was in or out of the court, giving no verbal call or hand signal. Do they think I'm a mind reader? Sometimes, they decide to make the call later as the game progresses. After I have assumed that the ball is good, my opponent announces, "Game's over." To me, if an "out" call is supposed to be instantaneous, doesn't it seem unfair that I have to ask, "Was that ball in or out?"

According to the rules, it is the player's responsibility on his or her side of the court to call "out" instantly and loudly, indicating with a pointed index finger if the ball landed outside the court of play. If the ball was in, a flat level hand symbolizes that call.

If you did not see the hand signal or hear the verbal call, it is perfectly proper to hold up your hand to halt play. Try to assume the positive and ask, "Was that ball in?" To enforce this as a habit, make the verbal call and the hand signal in social and tournament play.

● ● ●

I have a tremendous serve. My opponent can only block it back, and there it hangs above my head ready for my killing overhead. I suddenly hear him say that it was a "let." Then, when I start to question his call, his response is "I thought it hit the net. Play it over." It is highly unfair, since I know I had a winner "in my pocket." Should I put away the overhead and claim the point, or should I accept his call?

If a million dollars were riding on the point, I would call the USTA and cry that this rule is unfair. However, since the rules state that a player is to call an "out" or a "let" instantly, it still is his call, something you just have to accept. Crying and hitting your head against the net post are permitted but will not change the call.

Years ago I realized one stroke or one point does not decide the match. If a bad call has been made, it is up to you to work harder to rectify the call by hitting the next winner to make up for the error.

Tennis is a highly skilled and fun game. If you decide to wait for the perfect shot, the perfect game and the perfect opponent, it is possible that you may be playing very little tennis in the future.

● ● ●

What happens if I trip over a ball that was left on the court during a point? Is a "let" permitted if the wind happens to blow a ball from the fence onto the court?

If a ball is left on the court during a point, it is not only distracting to both players but also quite dangerous. If you trip over a ball, you will probably lose the point and could even end up with a sprained ankle. Also, be very conscious of balls scattered on the court during a practice session. In match play, if the ball in play happens to hit another ball on the court, the point will automatically go to the one who last hit the ball.

When my opponent fails to clear a ball from his or her side of the playing court, I will request that my opponent do so, before we continue match play.

If the wind blows a ball from the fence onto the court and I can see that it will be dangerous to my opponent or myself, I stop play and request a "let" (play the point over).

The same situation applies to balls from adjacent courts that roll onto our court. Winning by default due to an accident is never an achievement.

● ● ●

My opponent claims that he reached the ball and hit it after the first bounce. From my side of the court, I would swear that the ball bounced twice. How should this be resolved?

The rules state that the point goes to the opposing player: (a) if the ball bounces more than once before it is returned, or (b) if the ball touches any part of your body or attire, or (c) if in the process of hitting the ball, you touch the net. While you may think these rules are self-evident, a doubt may arise as to whether the ball bounced once or twice. In cases that are ambiguous, you just have to accept the integrity of your opponent.

If your opponent sincerely believes that the ball bounced only once, then accept his or her call. Of course, if there were an umpire, you know who would definitely be making the call.

● ● ●

My opponent has the habit of catching the ball when he feels it is going out of bounds. He claims that it is quite evident it is going out and catching it saves him the effort of retrieving the ball. What would the rules say about where you draw the line between balls that are far out of the court and those barely behind the baseline?

The rules state that a tennis ball is in play until it bounces out of the court. Touching the ball with one's hand or any part of one's body before the ball bounces out of the court (regardless of how evident it is that the ball is on its way out) is a point for the opposing player.

Remind your opponent of the rules by saying, "Don't catch the ball," and he or she will not be catching any nasty looks from you across the court! Given today's heavy topspin strokes or situations in which one plays into a strong wind, I am amazed by how an apparently long (out) ball finds its way back onto the court with inches to spare.

● ● ●

Should foot faults be called when friends are playing a casual match?

Foot-faulting is definitely against the rules. Unless they are clearly evident, I always find foot faults difficult to observe from the opposite side of the court. Most often, we have to rely on the honesty of the server to be aware of his or her own foot faults. Obviously, it is easier to notice foot faults when you are a spectator of other matches. Players with the problem are then marked with the reputation.

The simplest resolution to foot-faulting is to move six to twelve inches behind the line. If you put your forward foot on the exact edge of the baseline, you face the possibility of sliding onto and over the line. So, if you have a tendency to foot-fault, try moving back a little and think more about going up on that serve.

● ● ●

If my opponent is pulled wide on the court and cannot see the next shot (or his or her back was turned to the ball), who bears responsibility for making the "in" or "out" call?

The opponent normally should make all calls from his or her side of the court. If he or she asks you to make the call, be as honest as you can in your answer (even if the call is against yourself). After you have made the call, there should be no further questions. Your opponent is expected to accept whatever you say. All players, whether professional or amateur, are expected to place honesty and etiquette above all else on the tennis court.

● ● ●

I feel that my opponent has been making the wrong calls (known as cheating) on purpose. How do I resolve this type of behavior without sounding like a crybaby or a poor loser?

If you think the word diplomacy merely refers to our ambassadors' relations with foreign countries, allow me to enlighten you about reality. Situations of this type require a great deal of diplomacy. So shrug off the first and even the second bad call, since they may have been just honest mistakes. Keep the right attitude; after all, one bad call (or two) rarely determines the result of a total match.

Occasional bad calls have a way of equalizing themselves. If

your opponent happens to be a good friend, isn't your fun together worth a lot more than making a big fuss over a questionable call?

In tournament play, a player can always request a line judge. In a social match, a line judge is not necessary. In any case, you are safe in saying, "Remember that the lines count today," or "It must have missed by a hair." Also, try to keep a sense of humor.

You might take a more jovial route and talk about the time Brutus lost to Julius Caesar in tennis, claiming that Caesar cheated him on line calls: "They played on March 14th, and we all know what happened the next day...." Bottom line: If bad calls persist, refuse to play with this person again until he or she has read this book and realizes the importance of respect, fair play and tennis etiquette.

● ● ●

The bell just rang, indicating that the hour of indoor court time is over. With the score at deuce, the next hour's players are already waiting to come onto the court. Would it be inconsiderate for us to request that the new arrivals let us play out the last two points?

It is improper to make the request. Call the game a draw or decide to continue where you left off the next time you play. It is unfair to impose on the new arrivals, unless they suggest that you continue to play while they take out their equipment and get ready to play. Also, remember how anxious you were to begin playing when you had just arrived for your own court time.

● ● ●

I call a ball out, since in my mind I am at least 99 percent sure, but not 100 percent sure. So, why does my opponent have to look at me with that side glance?

The rules explicitly state that when there is any doubt, you have to give the call to your opponent. In a tennis player's vocabulary, the word barely does not exist, as in the following statements: "I barely touched the net," or "The ball barely missed the line."

Have you ever noticed how sensitive and lenient you are for the next series of calls after you have made a doubtful call? Shall we call this "guilt"? Be honest when making the call. By letting go of the lost point, you can concentrate better on winning the next one.

● ● ●

When I don't play well, I feel embarrassed, then humiliated. Finally, I begin to feel so stressed out that I end up playing worse than ever. Is there a way to break this pattern?

Everyone is familiar with a clown's performance in a circus act. The clown tries to be funny. When that does not seem to work, he or she tries harder, hiding any embarrassment behind a painted mask. The clown tries and fails, before finally realizing, "There's another crowd tomorrow and I'll do it better." And he or she does.

Treat your tennis game the same way. Do your best. By putting on a happy face, you will begin to relax and feel better. Playing badly is not the worst thing that can happen. Try to recall any amusing incident that makes you laugh or smile. Now take time to exhale, letting out a few deep breaths. Remember that if all else fails, there will be another match tomorrow. So, take heart!

● ● ●

During a match my partner keeps watching the players on an adjacent court. His lack of concentration on our court is very distracting to me. What is a subtle way to get his mind back onto our court?

Such distractions are common and can happen to anyone. An exciting point on the next court, an attractive person catching your eye, the annoyance of loud talking or laughter—all can divert our attention from the here and now. If the diversions persist, find out if another court is available to get away from the disturbance.

Explain to your opponent, "With so little time to work out, we shouldn't waste it watching the next court." Even if it turns out that no other courts are available, I believe that your opponent will finally get the "point" and start concentrating on the game at hand.

● ● ●

In the middle of a game, I have a bathroom emergency. Is it acceptable to halt play and take some time out?

By all means. Telling your opponent, "Time out! I have an emergency" is sufficient. Of course, it would be more convenient to wait, if possible, until you change sides. However, do not add to your mental and physical stress by delaying the call of nature.

● ● ●

On several occasions, I have seen men playing tennis without shirts and once in a while, professional players actually change their shirts at court crossovers. This appears unfair since women are not allowed to change their tops at courtside during a match. What is your opinion?

Shirts are mandatory on the court at most private clubs. I suggest always wearing a shirt when playing publicly. Of course, what you do on your own court is up to you. If a change of shirt is needed, ask for a time-out between games so you can change off the court, away from public view. While we may all be tennis players, more importantly we are human beings with personal pride and culture.

● ● ●

When I make court crossovers, is it necessary that I retrieve the balls and hand them to my opponent if it is his or her turn to serve? I don't want to lose my drink and towel-off time when changing sides.

In the allotted 90 seconds during which you change sides on those

odd-numbered games, you can towel off, take a drink or even take a catnap. If you want to be courteous and display good tennis etiquette, you can gather the balls and hand them to your opponent. In a way, it is like opening a door and holding it open for the person behind you. No one says you have to do it, but doesn't it make you feel just as good as the one who is coming through the door?

● ● ●

My opponent and I are late getting to our match and discover that the adjacent courts are already in play. What is the best procedure for getting to our inside court properly?

If the adjacent courts are in the practice (warm-up) phase of the match, it is acceptable to pass behind the players quickly with as little disturbance as possible. If they already have begun playing points in their match, wait inconspicuously on the side until the point has been completed. At this time, go ahead and make your quick dash behind the players. Whenever you move behind players, always be alert to avoid tripping over balls or being hit by a swinging racquet. I have been at private clubs where they request that players wait until a game has been completed before crossing. The idea here is that you avoid spoiling the players' concentration.

● ● ●

It bothers me when I am trying to concentrate on my match and another player from the adjacent court is ranting and raving loud enough to disturb me. What is the diplomatic approach to this situation?

Obviously, the player on the next court does not realize that he or she is affecting your game. So, at the first opportunity, approach the offending player when switching sides, but certainly not during a game. Be sure that your comment comes through as sincere: "I was concerned if everything is all right. Is there anything I can do to help?"

More than likely, the player will finally realize that he or she was disturbing others, feel a little embarrassed and then try to maintain better control. If we sincerely extend ourselves, I believe that we can truly help others as well as ourselves.

● ● ●

On occasion, I play with an acquaintance who holds a second ball in her hand after her serve is in play. Because of her two-handed backhand, she throws the ball either back to the fence or to the side of the court in the middle of our point. The movement of the bouncing second ball distracts me. She says that I'm making too much of a little thing and continues to repeat the action. Isn't this unfair?

You are right! Tennis etiquette says that it is unfair to have a second bouncing ball on or near the court to cause a distraction for an opponent. (In the How-Tos of Dressing chapter, I cover where to keep the spare tennis ball.)

If your opponent persists, do not be embarrassed to uphold the rules of the game, even if it means yielding the match and finding a new practice partner. In a tournament, be assured that the judge will rule in your favor.

● ● ●

A friend I play weekly has developed the habit of talking out loud to herself while the ball is in play. She says things such as "Kill it," or "Watch out for this one." She also tends to laugh out loud. This distraction has an unfortunate consequence. I lose my concentration, and that often results in my losing the point. Any advice?

Before your next match, take time to explain that while you do enjoy her enthusiasm, it has become a distraction that is affecting your concentration. Ask if she could try to contain her excitement until after the point, not during. As a friend she will understand.

The same holds true when playing doubles. During a point, try to keep lengthy conversations and cheers to a minimum until after the point has been made, so as not to distract your opponents.

● ● ●

Some professional players on television and local club players get so excited when making a crucial point that they put up a clenched fist. However, isn't the idea to excel against your opponent, instead of conveying the idea that the net is separating two pugnacious enemies?

I agree that excessively pumping one's fist after every shot won and constant outbursts of self-acclaimed excellence can seem offensive to an opponent, the players on adjacent courts and the spectators. Perhaps to the exhibitionist, it is a personally motivating gesture, but to the other players it abuses the essence of tennis etiquette.

When we play our sport, we never want to insult, intimidate or humiliate our opponent. Tennis etiquette basically requires that we show our opponent respect.

Avoid looking or acting obnoxious. Always try to exemplify tennis etiquette. You will discover that more people will be lining up for the opportunity to play with you.

● ● ●

When the weather is hot and humid, I find it difficult to hold onto my racquet. When I am sweating, the racquet twists in my hand, and I'm afraid it will fly off and injure someone. What's the appropriate way to handle this?

Except for the intentional throwing of the racquet, it really amazes me how seldom a racquet ever slips out of the hands of professionals as they strike the ball with all their might.

Here are a few options:

Some players keep a clean towel nearby so that they can easily wipe off the handle and their hands. If the towel is small enough, it can be tucked into your waistband.

You could also use drying powders, which are available for rubbing onto the grips. These can help to absorb excess moisture and also add a sticky feeling.

(Who can ever forget the sawdust and powder mixture that Ivan Lendl left scattered on the tennis courts when he played?)

There are also several types of tennis gloves on the market that provide a good grip. Some players keep several gloves in their bags so that they can alternate them as they become moisture laden.

Finally, for your own mental comfort, take note of the few times players actually lose their grip on their racquet.

● ● ●

What is your opinion of players who allow others to beat them intentionally on the court and seem to make a deliberate attempt to lose to a spouse, their employer or a client?

Frankly, I do not believe in throwing a match. The intent of every tennis encounter should be that each player tries his or her best; this way both the winner and the loser can walk off the court with pride and dignity.

Quality performers of all ratings want to play and win legitimately. They can always sense when someone throws a match, an event that can do more harm than good between the two players.

Après Le Match

Who closes the gate on the tennis court?

The last person on and off the tennis court is responsible for closing the gate.

Isn't a winner someone who wins the match? He or she walks away with the trophy, the prestige and the higher ranking, yet some claim there are more ways to win. To what are they referring?

Some players win a match by playing hard and within the scope of tennis etiquette. Others try to win by cheating, lying or conniving. Some players feel that they have won even if the score proves otherwise, because, along with doing their best, they have played with integrity, honor and pride. Often, a gracious loser receives more accolades from spectators than a winner does.

The competitive levels of play in tennis at all ages have imposed a tremendous compulsion to win at any price. This attitude takes the fun out of the game. Millions of people play tennis every year. Easily half of them end up losing, as far as the score is concerned, every time they play. However, every one of them can be a winner by having the proper attitude and trying to do his or her best.

● ● ●

I lost a match to a club player whom I can usually beat with one hand tied behind my back. As the word spreads around my club, how can I soften the embarrassment?

Losing is no disgrace. The best of professionals will attest to that. It does not matter if you have lost because of your health, the weather, court conditions or your lack of recent practice. The bottom line is that you lost. Accept the fact and praise your opponent.

Here is what the professionals may say after they lose a match: "I just didn't have it today," or "She played better today and deserved to win." To quell your concerns, I recommend that you play this person again. When you finish playing, win or lose, hold your head high and feel proud that you did your best. This winning attitude can soon change those smirks to smiles when you come off the court.

After I have played my match, what should I do with unwanted tennis balls? Should I leave them on the court or throw them away?

Unless you need them for your practice basket, it is proper to ask or look for the "Junior Practice Balls" box, which almost every club has. At a public court, I would leave the balls in their container at the side of the net. Some youngster will get a chance to use them. If your club lacks a "Junior Practice Balls" box, I suggest that you start one.

Speaking of what to do after your match, I am very careful about picking up and packing all my belongings into my tennis bag, even double-checking as I walk away from the court. It is also your duty to pick up your own trash before you leave (cups, bottles, cans, lids and so on). If you cannot find a trash can nearby, take the stuff with you. Respect the court and the players following you.

● ● ●

After an exciting match, I've seen winners jump over the net to shake hands with the loser. Why is this done and where did such a potentially dangerous practice originate?

Jumping over the net was prevalent many years ago when tennis was a much slower game and players had more stamina after the match. Today, players are totally exhausted from hitting hard and running themselves ragged; so, it is best to play it safe and avoid the risk of hurting some part of your body.

Injuring yourself after the match by jumping the net will put a damper on your celebration and make you look foolish. I suggest you meet your opponent at the net, extend your hand and give him or her a firm, sincere handshake. Also try to add a gracious comment such as "Great match. Thanks!" Doesn't this beat getting a broken leg!

I have heard this from professional male players and from men at our club: "I played so badly today! I played like a woman." How can I offset this sexist remark and the attitude it represents?

I do not believe it is necessary to waste any text on male chauvinistic remarks intended to dishonor female ability in life or on the court. People who make sexist remarks also tend to make other prejudicial comments that are aimed at embarrassing or degrading groups of people. Frankly, having to put someone else down to make yourself feel better shows very low self-esteem.

● ● ●

I find men still having a difficult time accepting a loss to a female on the tennis court. Gender should have nothing to do with an individual's talent and ability in a non-contact sport. How can women who play tennis diplomatically strike a blow against male chauvinism?

Back in the 1970's, Billie Jean King proved that gender equality does exist within the game of tennis. During a 3-out-of-5 set match, she beat Bobby Riggs soundly with a score of 6-4, 6-3, 6-3. This very big win for women has had quite a lasting influence.

Thanks to the great Billie Jean King and other female pioneers, women have come a long way. Today, most men accept women's equality in the tennis arena, although a few on the court as well as off still have a lot to learn. Such individuals force women to test the limits of their own ability to maintain proper etiquette!

● ● ●

I recently saw the completion of a championship final where the winner went to the net to offer the congratulatory handshake, only to see his opponent rudely snub him and storm

off the court in disgust. Isn't this type of action against the rules?

No, but impolite action of this type is certainly against any code of tennis etiquette. Obviously, while this player lost the match, he also lost the respect of other people, as well as a touch of class, defined by Webster as "a grading according to quality, value, superior attitude and elegance." Too bad that he squandered all of that by walking off the court without shaking hands. So, while not officially against the rules, this type of action was in poor taste!

● ● ●

I have seen professional players run up to the net after they complete a match. What do they say, and what is expected of me after a match and after a practice session?

At the end of a match, it is always proper to thank and congratulate your opponent. The good loser wishes the winner continuing success in the tournament. Here's a simple but gracious comment you might want to make: "No doubt, the better player won today."

The winner might say, "I lucked out today. You played great," or "It was a tremendous match. I'm looking forward to the next time we play." With close friends, you could say, "I really enjoyed it. Let's play again soon." Naturally, sincerity is important!

If we watch and copy everything else the pros do, why don't we consider imitating the conceding handshake and the victor's handshake, along with verbal compliments to each other?

After a practice session, I recommend trying the same response yourself. I am thankful to everyone with whom I play or practice, and I am pleased to tell them so.

● ● ●

I am tired of hearing excuses for why players, even some pros, lose in tennis. At our club, players will talk about why

they lost their match and come up with the wildest reasons: Here are a few of the more common excuses: "It was too windy a day for my type of game," or "My opponent was just lucky," or "My opponent played with one of those extra long racquets which threw off my entire game." Why does it seem so hard for some people to admit that they just did not play well or "have it" on that particular day and that their opponent played better?

Players in every sport tend to mentally rate themselves better than others. When a match reveals that they are at a different level, many players generate excuses. However, it is against tennis etiquette to make excuses that can detract from an opponent's enjoyment of his or her victory and enjoyment of the game.

TENNIS GREATS
SPEAK OUT

Cliff Drysdale

Winner of many singles and doubles titles including the U.S. Open (doubles). Original member of the Hampton Maid (traveling tour that included eight players who promoted world championship tennis). Finished in the world's top ten in singles five years.

It is so easy to become upset on the tennis court and lose self-control because tennis is a one-on-one, intense rivalry that few other life experiences can match. There is a clear-cut definition of winner and loser, which makes it all the more important to maintain tennis etiquette.

Jo Durie

Winner of many singles and doubles titles, including Wimbledon (mixed doubles). Ranked as high as number five in the world. Federation Cup and Wightman Cup player for Great Britain.

Tennis etiquette helps you to learn to control yourself in pressure situations. Also, you learn to appreciate the fact that your opponents are allowed to play good shots and that if they beat you, it is because they were better than you on that day.

Gus Bower

Betsy Nagelsen

Winner of many singles and doubles titles, including the Australian Open (doubles 2X). U.S. Wightman Cup player. Winner of the Chrysler World Doubles Championship.

Among the present players, I think that Monica Seles has exemplified extraordinary tennis etiquette both on and off the court. She has given points away after inaccurate line calls in her favor. Despite an awful lot of personal tragedies and distractions, she has been truly dedicated to the sport of tennis and supportive of worthy charities that surround the game of tennis.

In terms of past players, the gesture of Mats Wilander (when playing Clerc at the French Open some years ago) and his refusal to accept match point awarded in his favor because of a bad line call stands out in my memory as an extraordinary example of sportsmanship and appropriate tennis etiquette.

I think that it is unfortunate tennis players do not give their opponents points when unfair rulings are made in their favor, as much as they did in the old days. A few years ago, I was playing a doubles match at Birmingham with Larisa Neiland and was receiving serve on match point for us.

A serve was hit to me approximately eight inches out, and I reflexed the ball back to try for a winning crosscourt shot. When the chair umpire called game, set and match, Larisa, who stood at the net, turned to congratulate me. However, I told the chair umpire that the ball was out and that I couldn't win a match that way.

Our opponents served again, won the point and went on to win the match. I'm not sure whether Larisa was happy with me, but in my conscience I never could have won a match in that manner.

Tennis is like life. You have to be fair and play by the rules. You can't take an unfair edge.

Dick Stockton

Winner of many singles and doubles titles, including the U.S. Open (mixed doubles). Ranked as high as number seven in the world. U.S. Davis Cup player.

Except on Wimbledon's famed Centre Court, today's players hardly ever walk onto and off the court together. A beautiful tradition is just about gone from our game.

The traditional firm handshake at a match's conclusion is now becoming a meaningless gesture. No words of congratulation seem to be expressed, and players do not even look each other in the eye when they shake hands. Maybe they could shake hands when they gather at the net for the coin toss and receive instructions from the umpire. This would probably have more meaning.

Someone who has always exemplified everything good about tennis is Tom Gorman. He was always a good loser as well as a good winner, never making excuses for losing or for bad performances. He has always been a true professional both on and off the court. Most importantly, he has always had a great respect for the game.

One time, while he was playing Stan Smith in the semifinals of the Grand Prix Masters, Tom's back started bothering him. Tom continued to play. Eventually, he got himself to match point in the fourth set, but then defaulted the match, figuring there was no way that he would be able to play the final the next day. He did not want to win the set, only to default in the final.

Tom defaulted the match so someone else (his friend Stan Smith) would be there to play the next day. A pretty sporting thing to do!

Andres Gomez

Winner of many singles and doubles titles, including the French Open (singles). Finished in the world's top ten in singles three years. Ecuador Davis Cup player.

My parents taught me to use tennis etiquette not only on the court but also in life. Compete hard, try 100 percent, play within the rules and enjoy the game. Tennis has become a more "in your face" sport, similar to basketball or American football with a lot of showing off to your opponents or unnecessary fist-pumping at them.

When there is so much money involved and a "win at all costs" attitude, only parents can teach children how to become great champions, not only great winners. I have learned that professional tennis is played with umpires and linesmen and that they make mistakes, too. You have to play within the rules, which means that if the ball is out, it is out; if it's good, then it's good. You are taught that at home.

The Zen of Tennis

The player who most exemplifies tennis etiquette to me is Miguel Olvera, my teaching pro at the Guayaquil Tennis Club in Ecuador. He played Davis Cup, had beaten the U.S. in 1967 and had been the captain of the team. I think that he is still the most tennis-knowledgeable person I have ever known.

George Kaufman and Ralph Destino,
Southampton, N.Y.

CHAPTER FOUR
Doubles and Mixed Doubles

Doubles and Mixed Doubles

Doubles can spell t-r-o-u-b-l-e-s if players are not supportive of each other. Naturally, that is why it is so important to learn to communicate with, encourage and compliment your partner. Each of you must work together as a team. Enjoy the camaraderie and have fun!

The best "team" wins in doubles. As a team, it is necessary that you each know and anticipate the other partner's moves, timing, ability and attitude. The advantage of being a team is that you can help each other.

When you or your partner is feeling "down," the other will be there to pick him or her up. Always try to wear out the saying "Great shot."

It is helpful to put yourself into these real-life situations, which are represented in the following questions and answers. Note that they fall into two main categories: communication and doubles psychology.

Communication

My partner gets verbally offensive during a match, telling me what is wrong with my stroke and my play, including my judgment. Frustration enters, and the rest of the match goes downhill fast. What can I do?

First, never tear into any particular stroke during a match, since it is already too late for modification at that point.

It might be hard to accept this, but if your partner's typical play

is not to your liking, your evaluation should have come before you selected him or her as a partner. Meanwhile, make the best of it.

Second, just as following through is critical to a good stroke, so is "following through" with your partner. Think "positive" as you make an effort to encourage him or her with an affirming comment such as "Nice try. The ball was out but only by a smidgen."

Finally, try to focus on what has been working right for both of you as a team, especially in winning points. The important thing to remember is that winning a match takes a team effort.

• • •

My partner prefaces each point with: "We need this point! Just get it back." This added pressure distracts me, causing me to miss a shot and feel bad. Short of my smashing a good racquet or losing a partner, is there anything I can do?

Level with your partner: "Listen, I know every point is 'a big one.' Without the first, we can't make the second, the third, and certainly not the winning one. I'll try my best, but I do play better without your added pressure."

Suggest positive encouragement. A comment such as "You can do it" does more good than a negative one such as "Don't blow it." Remember, there is nothing wrong with a confident smile, a wink or a pumped fist accompanied by an enthusiastic "Go for it!"

• • •

My partner is a better, more experienced player than I am, but seems unsympathetic when I make a wrong move or wind up in the wrong place due to my "inferior" court judgment and know-how. I show my frustration since I am anxious to learn and improve. I realize that I am letting my partner down. What can I do?

Frustration is felt by the best and the poorest of players in all sports. It usually goes hand in hand with embarrassment, since we know

that we could play "better than that." After hitting a million serves, we wonder how we could still double fault at match point against the easiest player in the draw. (This often occurs when your friends travel great distances to watch you play!)

It is important to pick a partner that will complement your style of game. Being in sync with your partner will help relieve the unnecessary frustration, which is compounded when thinking you are letting your partner down. Talk up a match plan with your partner before and after the warm-up period. Discuss each other's strengths and weaknesses, as well as good and bad habits. Together, work on a strategic plan to win. This conversational give-and-take will help put you both at ease.

● ● ●

Our opponents throw a party whenever they win a point. Game play is always delayed by high-fives, excessive compliments and long discussions. We have just about had enough of their obnoxious, in-your-face attitude. What can we do?

Although communication and team support are mandatory during a doubles match, some players can go overboard with their excitement. This enthusiasm can be exasperating to opponents.

First, try not to create a delay between points. After each point, immediately move into position for the next shot. Second, if necessary, remind your opponents that play is continuous from the first serve until the last point of that game.

Try not to let their behavior affect your concentration. Focus on the ball and support your partner. Again, think "positive."

● ● ●

My partner calls a shot out, which I thought was in. How would you go about resolving this situation?

Such differences of opinion occur so often that there really should

be a special rule for this exact situation. Maybe the player nearest to the ball should prevail. If both players on a team doubt the call, then the points, without question, should go to their opponents.

I personally prefer that the player nearest to the ball make the call. Also, there is nothing wrong with asking your partner to make the call, especially if you were trying to concentrate on the ball and your stroke.

● ● ●

Our opponents are whispering and giving us the evil eye, even laughing at us. We feel intimidated. The match is bordering on meanness. Is there a way of escape?

You cannot escape. Remember that the concept of fair play means not interfering with the play of others, even the play of your opponents. You should try to be sensitive to the overall court atmosphere and make no one, except yourselves, the brunt of any jokes. If you cannot "take it," then why should the others? If your team becomes the victim of poor sportsmanship, assume that it is not personal.

Focus on your game and respond by playing harder, adding a polite smile and upbeat nod when hitting your next winning point.

● ● ●

Many female players at my club are complaining that some men are dominating the play during mixed doubles matches. Even when they have an easy put-away winner, they will hear the male voice behind them shout, "I got it." Is there a simple way to resolve this "hogging" before a duel of two racquets commences?

People can stretch the rubberband of politeness and congeniality only so far before it breaks and an explosion occurs. If one player is so weak or if one player is that strong, then each of you has picked the wrong doubles partner. (I personally have seen many females be the dominant power player and carry the team.)

Position on the court is the primary factor in deciding who has the first crack at the ball. I believe the person nearest to the net should go for the shot with the partner backing that person up, regardless of who is the stronger or the weaker player.

The time to make any changes from the normal position play is in team discussion prior to the match.

● ● ●

During our very first match together, my partner exposed a horrendous temper. Regardless of the score, all I heard was a barrage of bad language, needless yelling and unfounded complaints. I really felt embarrassed, since the behavior reflected on both of us as a team. How should I have handled the problem?

Several things come to mind for the "next" time:

- Request that the club post a sign at the entrance to each court or set of courts and put a notice in the club newsletter that foul language, yelling, complaining and disturbing the play of other members are forbidden. Such disruptive actions may result in the temporary or even permanent cancellation of one's membership.

- Support, praise and encourage your partner so that he or she is not "tempted" to have an obnoxious attitude. Sometimes, a bad shot or call happens, but do not consider it the end of the world. I tell my partner, "Stay cool. Things will turn around, and the points will soon be coming our way."

- On one occasion I told my partner, "Hold it down! I have my parents' picture in my tennis bag, and we certainly don't want to embarrass them." When all else fails, turn toward your partner and holding a forefinger to your lips, flash a forgiving smile and make the sound of the wind,

"shhh," which carries a world of meaning.

A true champion keeps emotions under control, is positive about winning and stays focused to achieve his or her goal.

Save your energy by giving your partner a copy of this book. You might kiddingly refuse to play again with your partner until he or she has finished reading (even mastering) it.

In fact, why not discuss certain chapters together?

Doubles Psychology

Sometimes I think my partner is going to get the ball when he thinks that I will. Once in a while, we have a train-wreck experience with both of us going head-on toward the same ball, our racquets swinging all over the place. Besides obtaining a confirmed hospital reservation, what doubles strategy do you recommend?

To win a point from an inexperienced doubles team, the old adage "Go down the middle" holds true. Why not take some basic lessons in doubles play since there is quite a difference compared with singles? Here are some fundamental differences in doubles:

- You will never wear down an opponent.

- Players at the baseline hitting ground strokes have an additional element to worry about—the "poacher." The poacher is the player who crosses over to his or her partner's side of the court and then manages to put the volley away for a winner.

- Play is crisper at the net, where most points are scored.

- Work both your strokes and your game toward the one who

is the weaker player and away from the stronger.

- Play as a team, allowing each player to make a complementary contribution to the joint effort.

- Work out a strategy with your partner. Try to be flexible as you discuss and alter your strategy while the match is in progress. Never feel afraid or embarrassed to communicate your thoughts as you progress through a match. It is appropriate before, during and after the warm-up to discuss your opponents, how you intend to handle them and your overall strategy.

Discuss your own condition ("Today my knee is hurting so you will have to cover me on . . . "), who will play on which side of the court and how you plan to handle shots down the middle. Again, I am an advocate of "nearest to the net goes for the ball first." The backup player does exactly that—backs up his or her partner.

By all means, communicate. Discuss what is happening on the court and get to know your partner's plans and ideas.

● ● ●

During doubles matches, the weaker player will often be looked upon as the "sacrificial lamb." The stronger partner becomes bored, and the weaker partner, who has been pummeled by balls, feels as if he or she is in front of a firing squad. What do you consider the best solution?

Accompanying the natural instinct to win should be the deep desire to win with honor, pride and enjoyment within the rules of tennis. Also, there is nothing wrong with attacking a weak stroke within the confines of your overall game strategy.

Similarly, you should plan a defensive strategy in order to neutralize such an attack and react accordingly if the weaker player has been under incessant attack. However, something is wrong if every shot is deliberately blasted at the weaker player just to win the point. This kind of tactic leads to boredom in the excluded player and understandable hostility in the player being attacked.

It is the better player who can execute his or her shot with control and clever placement, instead of with brute force. Now don't you think that this makes for a more interesting doubles match and a more congenial attitude on both sides of the court?

● ● ●

Sometimes I am more concerned about winning and impressing others than I am about having fun. As a result, my playing starts to wax pathetic. Instead of squeezing the racquet and hitting the ball, I find myself choking with my feet glued to the court. Help before I crawl into my tennis bag!

Nerves! Those long fibers connecting the brain and the spinal cord with the rest of our body affect us, especially when we walk in the spotlight. Even experienced performers start out with sweaty palms and a bit of nervousness. Actually, a little anxiety is good because it gets the adrenaline flowing and makes you feel excited and alert.

Here is a simple remedy that I use for relaxing: take several deep breaths, think of something funny (such as your opponent being naked), smile and let out a little laugh. This routine will send a signal to your brain that: (1) this is not a big deal, (2) errors in your game happen and (3) there is nothing wrong with laughing about it. Also, notify your partner of your mental diversion; otherwise, he or she will think that you have gone bonkers! Wouldn't it be great if that laugh of yours takes you all the way to the finals?

Incidentally, the warm-up period before a match is the opportune time to ease the jitters. It is true a little laughter can go a long way in putting a smile on your face and confidence back into your game. This approach makes for a better game, as well as for a more relaxing and enjoyable tennis experience.

During a doubles match when I've been making several conservative set-up shots, my partner moves in and tries a radical low percentage shot. The ball goes wild (or into the net). I stand speechless. What a wild shot to make after all the effort I put into setting it up! Sure, I could forgive his error one time, but my partner keeps repeating this performance over and over, leading to our losing the first set. How do I handle this without losing the entire match or my patience?

It is very important to realize that it is impossible for you to change your partner's game, stroke or showman's desire to be fancy. However, it is within your power to alter your game plan as you play the match. I personally like to point out to my partner that our opponents rarely can keep up with the conservative "just-get-it-back" game: "Let them beat themselves. We can be steadier than they."

Be encouraging. A smile and a "just out" comment can take you far, even though they hit the ball out by almost a foot. Everyone knows how easy it is to hit a bad shot. Every pro on the circuit can admit to having up and down days, good and bad games and even great and lousy shots in the same game. So, talk it up and wear out the saying "We can do it" throughout the match.

If the situation with your partner continues and you feel you are not complementing each other's game, I suggest leveling with your partner. Say something such as: "This is getting to be work without fun. Let's sever the partnership for future matches."

● ● ●

Our opponents hit a defensive lob that hangs in the air poised for a put-away overhead. Both of them are inside the service boxes, making it difficult to avoid smashing the ball right at them. Should I risk the point by finessing my shot between them or should I go at them?

Aiming to hit or injure someone is poor sportsmanship and a serious offense. Given no other alternative, I would smash the overhead at their feet. An even better shot is to angle the ball toward the sidelines with more finesse and less power. If the ball does strike an opponent, it is proper to make a sincere apology, as well as ask, "Are you okay?" Be sure to offer a short injury time-out, if needed.

● ● ●

Who is responsible for calling the serves in or out? What happens if the receiving doubles team has a disagreement regarding the call?

The receiving player's partner is in the best position to call all of the balls that go beyond the service line. However, the player who is the receiver is in the best position to call all of the balls wide of the center and the sidelines. If either player is in doubt, they have a right to confer. Just remember that if both are in doubt, the point goes to the opponent. In all cases, whoever makes the call should make it quickly, positively and loudly enough to be heard by all players.

TENNIS GREATS
SPEAK OUT

Angela Mortimer

International Tennis Hall of Famer. Winner of many singles and doubles titles, including Wimbledon (singles and doubles), the French Open (singles) and the Australian Open (singles). Finished in the world's top ten in singles ten years.

Etiquette on a tennis court or anywhere else is a matter of respect for both yourself and others. Once people perceive that you respect them, they should respect you in return. As a result, this reciprocity should help the wheels of life turn more smoothly.

Jim Pugh

Winner of many singles and doubles titles, including Wimbledon (doubles and mixed doubles), the U.S. Open (mixed doubles), the Australian Open (doubles 2X and mixed doubles 6X). U.S. Davis Cup player. Winner of the Miller-Lite International Tennis Hall of Fame Championship in Newport, R.I.

I compete by always trying to do my best. Regardless of whether I win or lose, I have a sense of dignity and respect for myself when I display proper etiquette during a match. My opponent's etiquette shows what kind of person he or she really is.

Also, it's fun pitting my skills against a competitor that I respect. It is never enjoyable playing someone who has poor sportsmanship.

Stan Smith

International Tennis Hall of Famer. Formerly ranked number one in the world. Winner of many singles and doubles titles, including Wimbledon (singles), the U.S. Open (singles and doubles 5X) and the Australian Open (doubles). Awarded the William Johnston trophy for outstanding character and etiquette on the tennis court.

My feelings about "tennis etiquette" revolve around the fact that I think players should compete as hard as they possibly can, while at the same time playing fair. By acknowledging your opponent's good shot, you give him credit and also take a little pressure off yourself. After all, the point was not necessarily lost by poor play on your part but by good play on his part. The bottom line, in my opinion, is that you should treat your opponent as you expect to be treated.

Wendy Turnbull

Winner of many singles and doubles titles, including Wimbledon (doubles and mixed doubles 2X), the U.S. Open (doubles 2X and mixed doubles), the French Open (doubles and mixed doubles 2X). Finished in the world's top ten in singles seven years. Voted "Sportswoman of the Year" by the Australian Press in 1983.

Proper etiquette is important in every part of our lives. We all need to know what is right and wrong and as a result live our lives accordingly. Proper etiquette teaches us to respect our fellow human beings, or at the very least, it should.

If all tennis players observed proper etiquette, not only would we enjoy our sport of tennis a great deal more, but our lives also would be a lot more fun and less stressful.

All it takes is a little thoughtfulness.

Left: Rachel E. Randolph
New York, N.Y.

Right: Averell Fisk
Palm Beach, Fla.

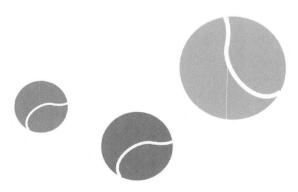

CHAPTER FIVE

The How-Tos of Dressing

"THE DRAWBACKS OF PLAYING IN TIGHT CLOTHES..."

The How-Tos of Dressing

People reveal a lot about themselves by the way they dress. What message are you sending with your style of clothing on and off the court?

You will be most suitably garbed if you purchase clothes that are specifically designed for tennis. Proper tennis attire has a simple style and is easy to move in. The most comfortable tennis clothes are made from cotton and other breathable fibers. They will keep you cool and are well worth the investment.

The following sets of questions and answers fall under three main categories: In General, Ladies Only and Gentlemen Only.

In General

Tennis apparel used to be based on elegance and style. Today's clothes seem to be more skimpy and tight-fitting for women and disheveled for men. Is there any chance of reversing this trend and returning to the days of "clean and basic"?

Fortunately, the "clean and basic" style will always be in fashion. It is most important that you wear properly fitting clothes that have a simple elegance and style. Many of today's tennis clothes for ladies include Lycra which will also give players the freedom needed to jump, twist and lunge, as well as look your best.

Can we ever hope to see more basics or softer transformations? All of the classics come around with a new little twist. In an ideal world, professional players would wear a set uniform as other professional athletes do without all the company logos and the excess of frills. It is up to you to set the example.

At my new club, anything goes as far as attire is concerned. Since I have just started playing, should I bother to buy new tennis clothes or just wear the running shorts and T-shirts I have?

What the other members do is up to them. If you commit to becoming a tennis player, I suggest you look the part with the correct clothes and equipment. Proper tennis clothes can be purchased at tennis clubs, sport shops and even department stores.

● ● ●

I dress up every day for work. When I play sports, I want to be comfortable and casual. What would be considered acceptable attire at the typical tennis establishment without getting too fancy?

You're in luck! The best in tennis clothes is not fancy. No designer logos are necessary. Tennis clothes should fit comfortably so that you can move freely and concentrate on playing your game. The quality of the material is also of key importance; so, buy what will last and still looks good.

● ● ●

Is there a dress code on public courts?

Unfortunately, there is no rule as to proper tennis attire on the public tennis courts. However, there is a rule for wearing proper tennis shoes and not street shoes. Even though the public courts have no formal dress code, I advise dressing smartly. You can purchase tennis clothes inexpensively. If you are interested in learning tennis and plan to play often, your small investment in proper clothes, a good racquet and a few lessons will pay off immediately.

● ● ●

I've been invited to play at a friend's club in Palm Beach, but the club has a strict rule about wearing white. So if I want to

play, I'll first have to purchase appropriate attire from a shop. Is this common?

Yes, this is common. A lot of clubs have a dress code to which they strictly adhere. When you invite someone to your club, always tell your guest if there is a dress code. If the host does not discuss it, the guest should ask. In any case, the guest is responsible for purchasing appropriate clothing.

● ● ●

I have just joined a club that requires all-white attire. If the clothes have a little color trim, is that passable? What about warm-up suits in the winter? Must they be all white?

Most clubs, including Wimbledon, do allow a minimal amount of color (trim on the collar, etc.). Usually, warm-up suits for the winter do not have to be all white.

● ● ●

I have been invited to play for the first time at a friend's house in the posh Hamptons. What should I wear?

It is important that you wear suitable tennis clothes and avoid jogging shorts or biking shorts. Simple and practical apparel is always chic. Alternatively, clothes that are subdued and fit properly are acceptable. Wearing white is a classic look that goes anywhere and has a natty appearance. If you are ever unsure of what to wear or what is acceptable, white tennis attire is your best bet.

● ● ●

Do I need to wear special shoes for tennis? How much does the court surface I play on really matter?

Shoes specifically designed for tennis are always acceptable because their light-colored soles do not mark up the court. Also, they do not have deep grooves on the soles like basketball or track shoes, which can tear up Har-Tru or clay courts. A shoe should be durable as well as comfortable. By the way, TENNIS magazine publishes an annual list of new shoes they recommend for quality and value.

● ● ●

My racquet cover is on the verge of bursting with all the necessities I need when I play. I am not fond of the suitcase duffel bags with crazy, psychedelic colors—their size makes me feel as if I'm carrying everything I own. Do you have any helpful suggestions?

You will know the right bag when you see it! You might try looking at the pro shop at private clubs if you want a smaller bag that looks more conservative. Many tennis clubs and country clubs tend to carry such bags.

Generally, for the more popular brands of clothing and equipment, look in the big sport stores. For the more conservative look, try the smaller boutiques and clubs. Tennis catalogs are also a good source. Considering the enormous array of sports bags around, be patient and in time you will find what really suits you.

Ladies Only

Is it all right to wear a golf skirt that looks like a tennis skirt?

Golf skirts are usually longer and more narrow than tennis skirts, which tend to be shorter and flare a little more to allow you to run, jump and not feel confined. Also, tennis skirts are more comfortable for playing tennis and are well worth the small investment. Tennis shorts are also practical and comfortable.

What is the proper length for women's tennis skirts? At times it may appear that some people either have a hot clothes dryer or are into a really hot agenda!

For women's tennis skirts, the proper length is the point at which you cannot see the tennis panties from a standing position. Some women want to wear their skirts shorter because they have great-looking legs. That is not always a matter of age but of genetics. A short skirt is not necessarily more flattering. Be smart and wear what looks most flattering to your figure.

Basically, shorts should be comfortable enough that you are free to leap and lunge through three sets. Besides having a proper fit, tennis clothes should always look neat and be clean.

● ● ●

Can women wear regular panties under a skirt? What is the benefit of wearing tennis panties?

Tennis panties are more desirable because they are more practical. They usually are made of 100 percent cotton, which tends to stay dry. Also, they may have pockets sewn into them for keeping a spare ball. The stretchy material will allow you to keep a ball next to your hip. You might prefer the more recent style of panties, which look more like shorts. Both are customary.

● ● ●

What is the most practical and acceptable way to wear long hair?

It is best when playing tennis to keep your hair off your face. You can accomplish this by wearing a headband or putting your hair in a ponytail. The latter style is the most common and is cooler on the neck. Basically, try to look like a tennis player, not a beauty pageant contestant.

My makeup runs when I get overheated. What should I do?

Most professionals do not wear much makeup on the court. One can be beautiful and natural with a clean, fresh look. Begin by wearing as little makeup as possible. Otherwise, when it is hot or you are sweaty, foundation can get spotty and even waterproof mascara can smudge. Always wear a sunblock. You can use one with a tint for a touch of color.

● ● ●

Where do I put a spare tennis ball? I have seen people put them in almost everything, from the pockets of shorts or panties to inside a shirt!

Women can put a spare tennis ball inside their tennis panty, right at the hip where it will stay secure. Some panties have built-in tennis pockets for balls. Tennis balls also can be placed in a simple device specifically made for holding balls conveniently at the waistline in the back section of a woman's skirt.

Putting a ball down one's shirt may be unique, but it is the least practical for tennis. For safety reasons, tennis balls should not be left on or near the court.

Gentlemen Only

What is the proper length for men's shorts?

For men, the shorter the length, usually the tighter the overall fit. If you have trouble placing or retrieving a tennis ball from the pocket of your shorts, this may be your first clue that the shorts are not so practical. Shorts for tennis should be comfortable enough that you can leap and lunge in them all the way through three sets. Besides fitting properly, keep them neat and clean looking.

A friend of mine shows up to play tennis looking like a rock star, half grunge and half neon sign. Everyone at the public courts is staring at us. How do I tactfully break the news to him that we are playing tennis, not going to a rock concert?

Try to go easy on him, unless the club where you are playing has a special dress code. If not, a disheveled, funky look is permitted. More importantly, you should set a good example of proper dress. Hopefully, he will soon catch on.

● ● ●

When the weather is hot and humid, I feel more comfortable playing with my shirt off. What rule do most clubs have regarding a man playing without his shirt?

Most clubs will not allow men, great bodies or not, to play without shirts. If the weather is hot and humid, remember to bring an extra shirt to change in to once you have gotten off the court.

● ● ●

What do you suggest as the most practical and acceptable ways for a man to wear long hair?

The most practical and acceptable way for a man to wear his hair is off the face. You can accomplish this by wearing a headband. Take a smart tip from one of the all-time tennis greats, Bjorn Borg, who had long hair and kept it in place with a stretchy terrycloth headband.

Who could disagree that Borg's overall appearance, tennis game and court conduct have always been impeccable?

● ● ●

Where do I put a spare tennis ball? Some men put them in

everything from the pockets of shorts to behind the baseline.

Many men find it most practical to put a spare tennis ball in the side pocket of their shorts so they can retrieve the ball easily. For safety reasons, do not leave tennis balls on or near the court when playing.

TENNIS GREATS SPEAK OUT

Don Budge

International Tennis Hall of Famer. Ranked number one in the world two years in a row. Winner of many singles and doubles titles, including Wimbledon (singles 2X, doubles 2X and mixed doubles 2X), the U.S. Open (singles 2X, doubles 2X and mixed doubles 2X), the French Open (singles) and the Australian Open (singles). First man ever to win a Grand Slam.

Etiquette, I have found, is important in tennis. If one wants to excel in the game, one should dress well. I've learned from our tennis camp days that when the kids dressed well, they always seemed to play better. Also, when they came in for dinner, they always behaved better.

All of the super players that I can remember never came on court unless they were neat and clean. Of course, sportsmanship is important. That goes along with dressing well. All the great champions that I knew were beautifully behaved and fun to compete against.

Pancho Segura

International Tennis Hall of Famer. Winner of many singles and doubles titles, including the U.S. Pro Championship (singles 3X and doubles 4X). Finished in the U.S. top ten in singles six years.

In my opinion, Stefan Edberg, the Swedish champion, was a role model of good tennis etiquette on and off the court. He never questioned calls given by the umpire or linesmen during a tennis match, and off the court was always a gentleman.

In the old days back in the 1950's, dressing properly also was a part of good tennis etiquette, whereas today the attire of lots of good players looks more like an unmade bed.

Jonathan Exley

Pam Shriver

International Tennis Hall of Famer. Winner of many singles and doubles titles, including Wimbledon (doubles 5X), the U.S. Open (doubles 5X), the French Open (doubles 4X and mixed doubles) and the Australian Open (doubles 7X). Finished in the world's top ten in singles ten years.

Tennis is a traditional sport that has made some modern adjustments to keep up with trends in pop culture. The sport, for the most part, is still presented best at a venue like Centre Court Wimbledon.

At the All England Lawn Tennis and Racquet Club, all of the players wear predominantly white, and there is no advertising by sponsors. The crowd is knowledgeable and polite. When you step onto the lawns in Section 19, you feel a higher level of respect and honor for the game. Throughout the years, I know that I have behaved better at The Champions than at any other tournament.

On television, some tennis players, especially Andre Agassi and the Jensen Brothers, have a greater appeal to a different audience than to the conservative, traditional tennis set that instead might more readily embrace a Pete Sampras or a Michael Chang.... Still, I think that the two groups can co-exist and help tennis reach a higher level.

Ken Rosewall

International Tennis Hall of Famer. Winner of many singles and doubles titles, including Wimbledon (doubles 2X), the U.S. Open (singles 2X, doubles 2X and mixed doubles), the French Open (singles 2X, doubles 2X) and the Australian Open (singles 4X and doubles 3X). Finished in the world's top ten in singles eight years.

Without the perseverance of the early pro-group of players, there may never have been open tennis. Many players of today do not understand this fact. So many changes have taken place in tennis equipment, court surfaces, technique and style of play, as well as in attitudes toward tennis etiquette.

Like manners, sporting instincts and etiquette begin in one's early days of development with family and continue as we learn from coaches and managers. Being an aggressive competitor should not affect court manners but be blended with good etiquette.

That leads to great respect from your peers. Don't stray from the tradition of tennis, mainly white clothing and coming on and off the court together as at Centre Court at Wimbledon. What a tradition of good etiquette!

Arley Koran and tennis professional
Julio Mejia, Acapulco, Mexico

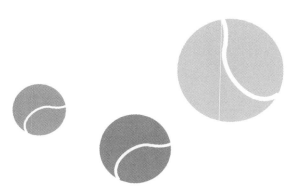

CHAPTER SIX

Taking Lessons from a Pro

Taking Lessons from a Pro

As a rule, most tennis instructors try to be patient and understanding with their students. However, instructors can lose patience when they feel someone is taking advantage of them or when they know they are being conned or treated unfairly.

The following true-to-life situations illustrate how you and your instructor can better respect each other and work together effectively. As a result, you will get more from your coach and your lessons.

I know someone who used the "I forgot my wallet" excuse, repeating the phrase several weeks in a row. That excuse was followed by "Oh, didn't I pay you last week?" What's your opinion of that?

It does look suspicious when a client repeatedly forgets to bring his or her wallet. If you tend to forget your money, try one of these options. Deliver the payment to your tennis pro later that day or leave it at the front desk in an envelope labeled with his or her name. If that fails, ask someone to pin a check to your collar.

Recently, I have heard that some instructors are providing clients with credit-card payment availability; others will work with a barter arrangement. Regardless of how you pay, just as practicing is your responsibility, so is timely payment for services rendered.

● ● ●

I have been with my tennis pro for many years. For several reasons, I would like to change coaches, but feel embarrassed

about switching. How do I handle this effectively without offending the pro?

Believe it or not, most pros are understanding. Never feel uncomfortable about telling your coach that you think you need a change of instructor or teaching style. Keep in mind that while he or she expects you to practice to be a better pupil and player, your instructor may also need to modify his or her own teaching style to be a better instructor. Losing you as a client is secondary. Of main concern is that you continue to play, to progress and to enjoy the game. If you do have to part, do so amicably, so that you will leave the door open if you should decide to resume tennis lessons in the future.

● ● ●

What should I do if I have to cancel a tennis lesson on the morning of the lesson? Once I had an emergency when a friend came in from out of town unexpectedly. I asked my instructor if we could postpone the lesson until the next day.

Your instructor probably was thinking the following: "As a busy pro, I've carefully planned for every hour in the day. Now at the last minute, you leave me hanging." To me, the word emergency connotes a dire emergency only. That is why it is important for a student to realize that he or she is always responsible for full payment to the instructor.

Most clubs and private instructors have a 24-hour cancellation policy. For whatever reason you have missed the lesson, if you did not give a 24-hour notice, it is still your responsibility to pay the full amount in a timely fashion.

● ● ●

After not having had a lesson in years, I wanted to polish up my game. By the end of my first lesson, the instructor had changed my style, grip, swing and attitude. At times, it

The Zen of Tennis

seemed that neither of us could decide whether I was right-handed or left-handed.

Communication between you and your instructor will make all the difference. Tell the instructor where you are having problems, what skills you would like to work on and what weak points you are most interested in improving.

Avoid that "everything" bit! Break it down into specifics. After all, "Rome wasn't built in a day," and the same goes for your game. Discuss your short- and long-term goals with your instructor.

Be realistic and start gradually, working up the achievement ladder one rung at a time. You need to have patience with two people: yourself and your instructor, who really does want you to succeed.

● ● ●

At the end of my lesson, am I expected to help my instructor pick up the balls? Isn't this included in the price of the lesson?

Proper instruction is included in the price of your lesson. After all, you would not want the instructor to use just three tennis balls during the lesson, which, of course, would make picking up the balls "no problem." That would balance out to be 90 percent ball pick-up time and 10 percent lesson time. However, with all the balls that the pro provides, you wind up with 90 percent lesson time and 10 percent ball pick-up.

You make the choice. You are hitting the tennis balls; therefore, you should help pick them up. On those rare occasions when my client explains that he or she has an emergency or is in a hurry, I will tell him or her to go and I will pick up the balls myself.

Sometimes young players feel that it is not "cool" to pick up the balls. More than likely, they also lack motivation. The really "cool" players are not ashamed to practice etiquette. They pick up the balls as fast as possible, get more out of their lessons and ultimately earn the label of "winners."

One instructor tells me one thing, while another tells me something else. How do I decide who's right and who's wrong?

It seems obvious that if a student gets advice from several pros, it is because that student was dissatisfied with the first pro in some way, whether his or her style, character, ability or attitude. Realistically, it takes time for an instructor to develop a good understanding of a student's game and a good rapport with the student. I suggest staying with only one instructor as long as possible. Absorb all that you can before moving on to another instructor, since this certainly will be less confusing and more rewarding to you.

You should be aware that there are many styles of teaching tennis. Each pro tends to emphasize a different area, such as footwork, consistency, physical conditioning or stroke production. Nevertheless, they all teach the basics. Here are four suggestions for selecting the best instructor for your situation:

- Stick with one instructor for a reasonable length of time. Give him or her time to understand your ability, evaluate your best qualities and prepare an improvement program. Do not jump from one instructor to another on a weekly basis. Avoid playing "hopscotch" with various pros and with your game.

- Evaluate the qualifications of your potential instructor. Does he or she display a thorough knowledge of tennis rules, proper strokes and, of course, tennis etiquette? What about his or her teaching technique? Also, ask yourself whether you both speak the same "language" (same level of understanding).

- It is best if your instructor has had some experience playing on a competitive level. He or she also should know various styles of play for different court surfaces, and be able to teach ways to avoid "choking" (performing ineffectively due to nervous tension during a match).

- Affiliation with a national professional teaching organiza-
  tion is a definite plus, although not mandatory.

What is most important is the honest and sincere rapport developed between you and your instructor. You are, in a sense, the extension of your instructor, just as the racquet is an extension of your
arm.

When you can respond comfortably to your coach's style, you
both enjoy the results. The bottom line is that you respect each other.

● ● ●

I am running 15 minutes late. Should my instructor extend my lesson a little bit longer? What if I am only five minutes late?

No matter what the degree of tardiness or how perfect the excuse,
you (and not the pro) are responsible for the lost instruction time. If
the pro can fit the make-up time into his or her schedule and the
court is free, he or she will accommodate your situation. However,
do not expect it. If "grace time" is offered, be appreciative.

● ● ●

My off-court activities are sometimes hectic and very stress-ful. So I often find it hard to slow down and relax before walking onto a tennis court to enjoy my lesson. Is there a for-mula for helping a casual player like me to get more fun out of the game?

Years ago, my father gave me an excellent bit of advice: "Take ten,"
meaning when you feel worn out, relax or take a ten-minute nap. I
believe that relaxation of the mind and the body would prepare you
to enjoy your play and have more fun. Try relaxing in a lounge chair
for ten minutes, maybe with soft background music. Set the mood

with deep breaths. Then slowly stretch each body limb separately and continue the slow, deep breathing.

As your body becomes more relaxed, concentrate on discarding all the stresses of your day. Then, when you pick up your racquet and begin to hit, focus once more on how easy, smooth and comfortable every stroke feels.

Enjoy the warm-up and you will enjoy the match. Even though tennis accelerates your adrenaline, it also can repress external stresses that are unrelated to your activity on the court. So, the real key is to relax and have fun.

Some tennis professionals practice rhythmic breathing to relax while playing. As the tennis ball approaches you, inhale slowly to the count of three and then exhale as you send the ball on its way.

● ● ●

Someone interrupts my tennis lesson to ask for a "moment" of my instructor's time. Five minutes have been lost, making me feel cheated. Shouldn't this time be added to the end of my lesson?

Not necessarily. Minor interruptions are common. There is the old adage: "Someday the sneaker will be on the other foot." Think back to the time you called your instructor to set up your first lesson. Did you interrupt him or her in the process of giving a lesson to someone else? In all respects, be patient and considerate.

Why allow 55 minutes of good instruction to be destroyed by a mere five minutes of selfishness? Every instructor wants you to be satisfied and may even suggest that you come in for the next lesson five or ten minutes early to make up the lost time.

On the other hand, if you find it absolutely necessary to interrupt a coach while teaching another student, I suggest that you try the following:

- Wait until the coach is picking up the tennis balls.

- Apologize for the interruption before asking the coach and the student for permission to interrupt with a quick question.

- Best solution: wait until the coach comes off the court.

● ● ●

My pro halted my lesson a few minutes early. I feel it wasn't fair.

Once the pro knows the student's skill level, he or she will set out to achieve specific goals in each lesson. Your instructor expects to have enough time to achieve those goals in a lesson, often by working on a particular technique over and over again. Normally, your instructor will not introduce something new in the last few minutes. So, utilize the end of a lesson by picking up the balls, cooling down and briefly reviewing what you learned.

Once again, may I repeat? If you are dissatisfied with how your instructor divides up the lesson time or with how you are progressing in your game, be honest and tell him or her.

● ● ●

Is it proper to tip my instructor?

Tipping is not required. Tennis professionals work for a fee and will provide a gracious service to assist you the best they can in improving both the quality of your game and your enjoyment of it. No pro should get angry for not receiving a tip.

If, however, you are pleased that the quality of service rendered is above the norm and would like to express your genuine gratitude, feel free to do so. Tips or gifts or other forms of recognition will certainly be appreciated. They inform the pro that you think he or she is doing an extra good job. I guarantee that your little gift will put a smile on the tired, sweaty face of your instructor.

As a beginner, I have an uncontrollable knack for hitting balls over the fence. In spite of my coach's urging me to slow down, the basket of practice balls dwindles quickly. What's really expected of me?

Let's first begin with the obvious. Of course, it is expected that you help to retrieve the tennis balls which went over the fence and those around the court. If you hit them, you should help pick them up. If you do manage to lose many of them, show a mature attitude by offering to replace them, even though your instructor will likely say, "Don't worry about it." Of course, you could compensate your instructor by taking more lessons and by eventually cutting down on that "uncontrollable" urge to hit the balls clear over the fence.

● ● ●

A friend of mine is a real "dinker." His entire game seems to revolve around slices, lobs, drop-shots, spins and blocking shots. Many players refuse to play with him because of his unorthodox strokes. Should I tell him what others think of his game or just avoid all comments?

In the early beginnings of the sport, the "dinker" style was popular. Gradually, the "dinker" lost out to the "smasher," as styles and racquets evolved. Suggest that your friend take lessons from a pro so he can develop a topspin forehand/backhand and also add power to a first serve. It will turn him into a very good player.

Anyone who refuses to play against a dinker does so because he or she knows that the dinker's simple style is difficult to beat. The dinker forces an opponent to work a little bit harder for every point. Dinkers also make great practice partners because they keep you on your toes and force you to play more more consistently. Being familiar with different types of play and strategy can be a good experience whether playing socially or in tournaments.

In spite of my friend's professional attire, attitude and tennis knowledge, she has a major flaw in her game. Bluntly, it's her bizarre and unorthodox strokes. I know a few lessons would really help her. How can I introduce the idea to her without losing a friend?

Enthusiastically explain to your friend how lessons from a pro have really improved your game. Suggest, even insist, that she take a few lessons from your pro. If it happens to be her birthday or because she is your friend, give her one or two lessons as a present. P o i n t out that lessons will lift her game to a championship level. If she still insists that she is satisfied with her game, break the truth to her firmly but gently: "When you improve, we both will be better. I've spent a lot of time and money to play better. If you and I are going to continue to play, I expect that you sacrifice a little in time, effort and money to join me. We're great together; so let's do it."

● ● ●

It's only recently that I got interested in tennis, and everyone is overly anxious to instruct me as to what is right or wrong with my play. Unfortunately, one person contradicts the other. I don't know which way to turn or how to play. Their intentions are good, but I would rather be left alone to decide for myself. What should I do or say?

Whether you are a novice or an intermediate player, everyone will have "some advice" to give you, especially after they have seen you do something in a "questionable" way. First, thank the advice-giver graciously. Then, put the comment in the back of your mind for a later discussion with your pro. Next, if you have no instructor, discuss the situation with other players and get their opinion. Finally, give some weight to all comments, but do not dwell on them for long. By taking lessons from a pro, you cannot go wrong, since he or she will guide you along a slow but proper path to playing the game correctly and will be there to help you when you need it.

Another benefit: A pro can identify your weak points and strong qualities and thus help you to pattern your game accordingly.

● ● ●

My instructor keeps telling me to read as many tennis books and magazines as I can. She claims it would help improve my game and also teach me tennis etiquette. True or not?

Absolutely true! I advocate reading literature that will expand and improves one's mind and self, tennis included. Information on our sport gleaned from articles and books can be invaluable. For example, a four-dollar magazine can give you secrets learned by pros from years of experience. These same tips cost as much as $100 an hour per lesson. Best of all, the same magazine breaks down the mechanics of a stroke and features a variety of styles and techniques, one of which might suit your particular style of game.

Through a book, an instructor can relate a lifetime of incomparable experiences that can go in depth for your benefit. These often convey the respectability and elegance of both the individuals and the sport. Why would anyone want to read about how uncouth and nasty some players can be on the court? By reading about the opposite, you will learn about tennis etiquette and its attributes.

● ● ●

Is it necessary for an instructor to repeat what I already know?

So often when a pro is teaching, the student will respond with the words "I know." This comment can be rather frustrating for the instructor, whether he or she is showing you something new or just reminding you of something you already know.

The fact is that had the pro seen you doing it correctly, he or she would not be telling you. So the next time you catch yourself saying

"I know," keep in mind that you really do not know or else the pro would not be correcting you!

Tennis is all about repetition. There are only so many strokes in the game, but we must practice them as much as possible. Through constant repetition, the pro is instilling in you what is proper so that you will begin to play without thinking. In other words, when you know it well, it will become second nature.

An instructor may say the same thing in several different ways, one of which might "click in" better and thus help the message to eventually get communicated and achieve good results.

TENNIS GREATS
SPEAK OUT

Zina Garrison

Winner of many singles and doubles titles, including a gold and bronze medal in the Olympics. Finished in the world's top ten in singles seven years. U.S. Federation Cup and Wightman Cup player.

I have always felt that it was right to have good sportsmanship. You must play the game well but not disrespect the person you are playing. Trying to win any way will catch up with you. Playing the game with the rules in mind is the only way to win respect in the end. Being able to look at yourself in the mirror after anything as well being able to like yourself is the sign of a true champ, knowing that you played fair. That is a champ in life.

Gene Mayer

Winner of many singles and doubles titles, including the French Open (doubles 2X). Finished in the world's top ten in singles two years in a row. U.S. Davis Cup player.

Tennis etiquette is not merely a set of archaic standards of expectation for behavior related to tennis. It is just as important to the enjoyment of the game as the rules are. Adherence to the rules can make the match comply with international regulations. However, it does not guarantee one's enjoyment, which comes from the simultaneous utilization of tennis etiquette and rules.

Some examples of important rules of etiquette that greatly impact the game of tennis are: The server controls the tempo of play, while the receiver makes every effort to comply. Calls can be verified but not continually questioned. Try to differentiate normal ready positions from attempts to interfere with the server's concentration.

All in all, tennis is an exciting sport that can be seriously hurt by the obliteration of etiquette.

Tony Trabert

International Tennis Hall of Famer. Ranked number one in the world two years. Winner of many singles and doubles titles, including Wimbledon (singles), the U.S. Open (singles 2X and doubles), the French Open (singles 2X, doubles 3X) and the Australian Open (doubles).

Stefan Edberg was, and still is, very dedicated to tennis. Ranked number one in the world in singles for 1990 and 1991, Stefan has won eight Grand Slam singles and doubles titles. He also played Davis Cup many years for his country, Sweden.

More importantly, he has always been a gentleman and a sportsman. Both on and off the court, he has represented himself, his family and the wonderful sport of tennis perfectly.

Any sport would be proud to have him.

Billy Talbert

International Tennis Hall of Famer. Winner of many singles and doubles titles, including the U.S. Open (doubles 4X and mixed doubles 4X) and the French Open (doubles). Finished in the U.S. top ten in singles 13 years. Awarded the William Johnston Trophy for outstanding character and etiquette on the tennis court.

At Wimbledon, one can read these lines from Rudyard Kipling upon entering Centre Court: "If you can meet with Triumph and Disaster, treat those two imposters just the same...."

Tennis etiquette is a code of conduct that can be used in sports and in life. It teaches one how to accept triumph with modesty and how to address defeat with respect for one's opponent and quiet determination to do better the next time.

Tennis etiquette also embodies both patience and the ability to believe in yourself, despite disappointments. A true champion in life or on the tennis court will always play by the rules.

Left: Mark Albom
New York, N.Y.

Right: Blair Albom
New York, N.Y .

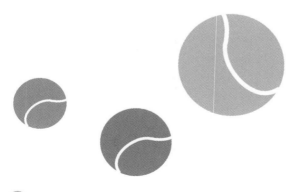

The Zen of Tennis

CHAPTER SEVEN

Pointers for Parents and Their Kids

Pointers for Parents and Their Kids

For tennis to remain an active, interesting sport that attracts quality participation, we should introduce tennis and tennis etiquette as early as possible to young people. In addition to enhancing the development of body balance, motor coordination and self-confidence on the court, tennis and tennis etiquette provide many advantages that will affect our daily activities off the court in a positive way. One of etiquette's many benefits is helping young people develop the ability to successfully work and associate with others.

While it is obvious that the challenge of tennis and the physical and emotional intensity experienced on the court often do parallel our daily work and school environments, learning tennis and applying the rules of etiquette ultimately expose the student to the fraternal order of true sports people, that elite group who, by tradition, personify honor, kindness, generosity and courtesy.

I cannot overemphasize the important role that parents play in their children's learning of tennis and tennis etiquette. If you are a parent or a young person old enough to play tennis, reading this chapter will be beneficial to you both on the court and off.

Join me as we present the following situations that will help you in understanding the dynamics of tennis etiquette.

• • •

How can I best teach my children about tennis etiquette?

By *exemplia docet,* Latin for "teach by example." There is no better example than for you as a parent to be a paragon of etiquette. Of course, the instructor has the responsibility of teaching tennis etiquette in his or her lessons. As you read this book on tennis etiquette, why not take the time to discuss the concepts with your children?

● ● ●

Is there an important safety rationale for practicing tennis etiquette that applies to both children and adults? If so, can you please give me some clear-cut examples?

Definitely yes! Several safety reasons come to mind:

- Remove a ball from your court before putting the next ball in play. This will prevent you from tripping over the ball or your own feet as you try to avoid the ball.

- Wait to cross courts until after a point has been played. This way you can avoid being hit by the ball and the flying racquet of a player who cannot see you behind his or her head.

- Be careful to avoid hitting an overhead smash directly at an opponent right in front of you close to the net. Needless to say, eye damage or a broken nose is never worth winning a point.

- Avoid making bad line calls, unless you want to be responsible for contributing to a heart attack when you drive your opponent into a rage.

● ● ●

Are there any incentives or awards for learning, practicing and promoting tennis etiquette?

I have seen several clubs present awards (trophies, plaques or certificates) to their members for the practice and promotion of tennis etiquette. Recipients are recommended by club members based on performance on the court or around the club during indoor or out-door seasons. On occasion, an award will be presented for special service rendered to youth or senior programs.

My hope is that, in the future, more awards will be given for sportsmanship at tournaments to those deserving of the honor. Players and tournament officials could make the nominations.

Probably the greatest motivators in learning and practicing tennis etiquette are personal pride, honor and respect, which form an attitude that is welcomed everywhere in the world—from the fanciest of clubs to a friend's backyard court.

● ● ●

I have noticed that tennis instructors seem to focus most of their time on teaching strokes and strategy and rarely, if ever, on tennis etiquette or good sportsmanship. Sometimes, the result is talented youngsters who behave like spoiled brats. Because etiquette is so important in regard to the issue of safety and proper behavior, how can concerned parents convey its necessity to their child's instructor?

Very simply, parents should request that tennis etiquette be taught in the programs in which they enroll their children. Instructors are generally reluctant to bother with etiquette for several valid reasons. Etiquette does not produce immediate results, such as a better forehand, which the parents are more anxious to see.

Etiquette also involves an emphasis on discipline, which sometimes children resist. Usually, parents are the first to hear about an instructor who reprimands a child. Some pros may want to avoid a confrontation. However, it is the parent's responsibility to find and encourage a pro who will take the time to incorporate etiquette into their lessons. When your child stops taking tennis lessons, etiquette will be remembered, and its long-term effects will be more beneficial than proper stroke technique.

Most important of all, parents, the etiquette you practice off the court reinforces the etiquette your children learn in their lessons!

Before every tennis match, my youngster becomes quite irritable and nervous. If he loses the match, he feels so down emotionally that he will pout for a week. How can I help to relieve the pressure initially and later lessen the pain?

All too often, youngsters needlessly pressure themselves into a "do-or-die" attitude. If they fail, they seem to die mentally, thinking that their peers will consider them losers in everything they do. This is why parents and coaches need to emphasize that all they want and expect from children is that they do their best when competing in sports, at school and in everyday life.

A child may lose the match and feel like a loser. That is why it is so important for us as parents and coaches to emphasize that losing or even winning a match is not the predictor of success or an indicator of one's value as a person. Children need to learn that almost every player who faces a Lindsay Davenport or Pete Sampras across the net may be a loser of the match, but he or she can also be a winner because it was a privilege to play these pros. Losing gracefully is a skill a child needs to learn both on the court and off.

No young person ever walks onto a court with the innate ability to be a champion. Through desire, practice and proper guidance, anything is possible. Many individuals have achieved success through their steadfast dedication to improving in the face of insurmountable obstacles. You can instill this mind-set in your child's own outlook toward sports and all human endeavors.

Some parents who think that their child was "robbed" of a win sometimes belittle the opponent or make the child think that he or she played well, even though it was obvious that their child did not try his or her best. The worst thing a parent can do is to make weak excuses, such as "Your opponent just had a lucky day."

Most people of all ages play tennis because they love the game. Only a very small percentage of people will play professional tennis for money. Consequently, why should a child be upset to the point of having a nervous breakdown because he or she lost a match?

Parents need to emphasize to their children that they will always be a winner in their court. Being a winner means accepting the fact that they lost a match without blaming anyone, including themselves. A real winner gives his or her all and learns from every experience in spite of the actual score.

Finally, remind your child to get out there and have fun, including laughing at his or her own dumb shot or stupid move. When playing tennis, as well as in everyday life, you will create more satisfaction, happiness and success if you learn to enjoy the process. If we can teach kids to let go of their concern about the outcome (feeling they must win all the time) and to not fault themselves for their mistakes, it will make all of their endeavors in life easier for years to come.

● ● ●

A nasty rumor has gotten around the tennis club that my child has been cheating on calls. While I am naturally defensive, in all fairness I feel that I must look into the situation. What should I do?

Immediately initiate a parent-child discussion that focuses on what has caused the initial accusation. Follow it up with an explanation of the essence of tennis etiquette. As you foster an atmosphere of true sportsmanship, emphasize just how important it is for your child to give opponents the "benefit of the doubt" on calls.

Explain to your child that you are wiping the slate clean of past transgressions and that you expect him or her to begin with a new attitude in which personal pride and the desire to have fun are most important. Clearing the air will alleviate the psychological pressure of winning at all costs. Also, drive home your support and satisfaction with lots of praise for him or her, regardless of the score.

On the other hand, perhaps your child is not at fault, in which case you should discuss the situation with the instructor.

The Zen of Tennis

I often hear parents complain that when they enroll their youngster in a tennis class or clinic, the instructor shows favoritism to a choice few. Usually, these are the students who have been with that instructor in several previous classes. If everyone is paying the same fee for the lessons, please help me to understand why the instructor is giving more attention to some and less to others.

Often, when tennis instructors provide information or give a demonstration, they tend to present it to the entire group. A good coach will also direct specific comments toward each student's particular needs, in addition to the general comments.

The longer a student takes lessons from the instructor, the more likely it is that the instructor knows the student's game well enough to make detailed comments. If the coach needs a model during the lesson, it is natural to select a student whose abilities are more familiar to the pro. Usually, an instructor will give more attention to the students who require more skill-building, rather than to the student who is doing exceptionally well.

Still, every student in a class is of equal importance and deserves equal time. If you or your child feels a bit shortchanged, go to the pro and discuss your grievance. There is no need to feel intimidated by your instructor. His or her main objective and desire is to help you.

● ● ●

After returning home from a tennis class, my child complained that the instructor had singled him out to mock him in front of his peers. He now feels embarrassed in the class and is resentful of the instructor. What should I do to remedy this situation?

Throughout my years of teaching tennis in both schools and private classes, I have found that every student (regardless of age) feels nervous and worried about his or her performance. Every student wants to

impress the instructor and his or her peers.

If a student does poorly and the coach tries to correct his or her performance, the student may often take the correction personally or think that the coach was out to embarrass him or her. Students need to realize they are part of a group and must work together.

Instructors typically use students in the class to illustrate various points. They have no interest in discouraging students by making them the butt of a humorous remark or by commenting on their form or play just for the sake of hurting them. If necessary, I see nothing wrong with the parent, or preferably the student, pointing out that they dislike the way the instructor made the criticism. The parent and the student should feel free to request that the coach "please refrain from making an example" of the student's faults in front of the class.

On the other hand, everyone will occasionally make mistakes in his or her game. Having someone gently but firmly point them out is the only way to correct those errors.

Someone is bound to hear the correction, since most classes are conducted near other adjacent courts. The end result is that you will benefit from the correction. After all, isn't that what you want the instructor to do: help to fix whatever you are doing wrong?

● ● ●

Recently, I made a surprise visit to my child's tennis class and found the group to be completely out of control, with screaming, wild laughter and confusion everywhere and very little, if any, real tennis being taught. Considering the cost of tennis lessons, shouldn't there be better control? Who is responsible?

No doubt, all clubs should have some standard for proper behavior. Unfortunately, poor behavior will give a club, as well as a pro, a bad reputation. When an instructor walks onto the court, that individual has the responsibility for his or her student's behavior. It is also important to maintain control not only for the sake of learning, but also to show respect for the players on the adjacent courts.

Occasionally, I hear the flimsy excuse that "the youngsters have to let off steam" or "we want them to have fun." I do not subscribe to this attitude. Full control of the class is necessary in order to provide a proper learning environment.

If the pro is relaxed and having fun, his or her attitude will set a good example to the students. I am a firm believer that good behavior is not inconsistent with fun.

● ● ●

Tennis coaches are normally selected because of the talent they display on the court. Sometimes we overlook their attitude, appearance or lack of responsibility on, as well as off, the court. I am really concerned that vulnerable young students will become victims of their instructors' bad qualities. What can be done to avoid this?

Both good behavior and bad behavior are contagious. Why expose your children to the latter in tennis instruction? There are plenty of tennis coaches who not only are excellent players but also proudly set the example of tennis etiquette and display good behavior both on and off the court.

Tennis coaches are responsible not only for themselves, but especially for their students, who must be taken care of properly in a professional manner until leaving their coach's supervision and arriving home safely.

Interview potential instructors and, if possible, observe some of their classes before you make your selection.

● ● ●

Is there any good reason for a tennis instructor to dislike it when parents are on, near or within hearing distance of a tennis court while students are being taught?

A couple of reasons come to mind. The instructor may feel that his or her teaching approach is unique and would not want it copied by others. Also, he or she may feel that having parents on the sidelines is a distraction, which can interfere with the learning process. During a lesson, an interruption such as "good shot" can do more harm than good to a student's concentration. I have heard pros request that parents on the sidelines be quiet if their comments or conversation were much louder than their own. If parents adhere to proper etiquette, I cannot imagine why the instructor would object.

A parent's presence on or near the court is a strong sign of support for the student. It is also a way of helping to prime a student to play before future spectators. Who can argue with that?

● ● ●

In the process of maintaining class control and discipline, does the tennis instructor have the right to scream, shout or push the students to extremes, even to the point of tears?

There are a variety of styles of class control and teaching: (1) the gentle approach, which tends to appeal to the more mature students who are out to absorb as much as they can in a short time; (2) the more rigid, stern approach, whereby the students are pushed to the point of utter exhaustion or disgust; and (3) the in-between approach.

I like to compare this second style to that of an army sergeant or college football coach who barks commands to toughen up the group and get that extra ounce of effort out of them.

Then there is the instructor who screams, rants and raves at the top of his or her short-lived voice. This type of instructor appeals only to those students who are able to mentally turn off their hearing after the first sentence. They also must be the ones who enjoy watching the instructor waving his or her arms wildly and jumping up and down.

These students develop a sensitive on/off closure valve in their ears (which is mentally controlled) or they come to class secretly prepared with earplugs. You can easily identify them, since this is the group that usually says, "Huh? What? Where? I didn't hear you!" after the instructor has ranted and raved for the first ten minutes.

Students should never leave the class crying or hypnotically staring into space. Actually, it is not necessary, and is even quite detrimental, to the learning process to push a student mentally and physically to the extreme.

The third approach belongs to the "in-betweeners" who combine a little of each style. The instructors usually modify their teaching style to suit the type of students in the class, going crazy when both styles are required in the same class.

Parents and students, I pass the tennis ball back to you. Do some research and select the instructor with the style best suited to your situation. There are plenty of pros who teach in a style that should make you both feel comfortable.

● ● ●

The only time I have to play at my club is in the late afternoon. Often this is also the time when most junior programs are in the process of holding classes. The distraction of noise and errant balls is a serious problem. Is there a solution to satisfy everyone?

Unfortunately, due to mandatory school hours, the only time most junior tennis clinics and classes take place is in the late afternoon. If your club has enough courts, request they schedule you on a court that is away from the juniors.

An emphasis on tennis etiquette by instructors in these junior classes also would help to improve the "sound" situation.

I am taking lessons from a well-known professional instructor. Also, I get lessons from my parents, who can't resist coaching me. Now I feel confused because my parents and the instructor use such different methods. While I prefer the pro's style, I don't want to offend my parents, who are paying for my lessons. Help!

That irresistible urge to coach others, especially one's own child, is called "parental interferiditus," the disease of parents thinking they know more than the professional coaches they hire.

It is an absolute rule that there should be only one coach teaching a subject. Not until the pro has transmitted his or her stock of knowledge should a change of coaches be made. As all master chefs would agree, "Too many cooks spoil the broth." Having more than one instructor not only will take away the fun but also will drive the student far from the sport. Surprisingly, even the professional tennis-playing parents, who might still be, or once were, masters in their sport, usually prefer to have another coach work with their child. This should be the rule, unless it is a matter of economics and the parent truly has ample time and patience.

Parents need to discuss with the instructor the topic of helping in their child's tennis development. This will prove helpful to both child and coach. Begin by asking, "What can I do to help my child's progress and thus assist you? Are there any specific drills I could work on with my child?" A good instructor will appreciate a parent's sincere help and be reassured that the student is practicing properly.

Time with your child will be more enjoyable without the built-in stress factor of another instructor. Parents should encourage their child to read the many information books and view the helpful videos on the market. As questions arise, parents should always ask their child's instructor for helpful advice. Remember, staying "apart" from the coaching job will keep parents "a part" of their child's life.

Is there a problem with asking my child when returning from a tournament, "Did you win?" He either sadly goes to his room without so much as a word or bursts out with the comment "Is winning all you ever think about?" Is my concern unfounded?

Timing, good sense and diplomacy are always all-important factors between parents and children. Most parents send their children to learn tennis in order to have a lifetime of fun playing the sport. It is important that you stress pride, honor, fairness and respect—tennis etiquette. However, this message will be lost the minute your child returns from a match if your first question is "Did you win?" Even though you do want to know if your child won, decide on the best time.

As a parent, you know how your offspring feels simply by looking at him or her. How different it would be if you were to change the approach and open with, "Hi, champ! Maybe now's a good time for a nice, warm shower. We have something special for dinner. Afterward, you can tell me how you played today."

Later on, ask other questions such as: "Did you have fun? Have you tried that new serve you were working on? How did you feel about your game?" Bring up the fact that your child is never a loser if he or she had fun, did his or her best and learned something from the match. The recipient of the second-place trophy at the U.S. Open is always a loser, and I sure "wish it were me."

● ● ●

At a tournament, is it acceptable for me to applaud my child's opponent when he or she executes an excellent shot?

Most savvy spectators are not conspicuous. They applaud at the correct time, such as when a point has been made with extraordinary finesse, even if won by their child's opponent. Of course, it is always proper to congratulate the players at the end of a match with diplomatic words, such as "Great match" or "A pleasure to watch."

● ● ●

Where can I find an approved tennis program for my child— one that teaches not only the fundamentals but proper etiquette, too?

Try contacting the USTA (United States Tennis Association, White Plains, N.Y., telephone 914-696-7000) and request programs, along with a sectional contact in your area. You can obtain additional information by calling local tennis clubs (check your local telephone book) and by looking in newspapers or magazines.

Often, counties and local community groups will provide tennis classes, which go from beginners through advanced tournament players. How well the programs are taught or what emphasis they place on etiquette is something else for you to research. (Note that I have covered how to select a private tennis instructor in chapter 6, in case you decide to follow that route.)

● ● ●

At what age is it best to begin teaching a child tennis? If a child has trouble in the beginning hitting the ball, should he or she stop playing to avoid disappointment?

It is never too early, never too late to learn tennis. Every age can be the best time to learn to play the sport. Great players have surfaced from childhood tennis players who could barely hold a ball in one hand. Also, I have had the pleasure of giving lessons to terrific students who were over eighty-five (yes, 85) years young.

Regardless of one's age, learning to play tennis is a slow process that requires extensive practice time. A new student needs proper instruction to avoid bad habits and lots of encouragement from parent and coach. Stressing the fun aspect will keep children involved in the sport and jump-start their development. After all, everyone enjoys participating in things that are fun.

My child has shown a sincere interest in tennis, but lacks that "above all else" desire to improve. Is my parental pushing helpful or harmful to my child?

As with cough syrup and a lot of other things, a little may be good; however, a lot can be bad. Motivation in moderation and sincere encouragement offer the best approach for you as a parent to follow. You want your child to enjoy the game while learning not to rebel.

It is essential that you allow your child to develop, from his or her coach and peers, that drive to excel.

Losing a match to friends can be enough to motivate your child to start working harder and improve his or her game. More importantly, you as the parent will remain the "good guy."

● ● ●

I have heard youngsters complain that tennis etiquette is emphasized in their programs, yet some older players exemplify the worst sportsmanship imaginable. Why is this?

The need for tennis etiquette has no boundaries. It is required at all levels by players of all ages. You do not reach a certain level of play or get to a certain age and automatically have perfect etiquette.

Yes, it is possible to win matches with poor tennis etiquette, but invariably, these players always appear miserable and often they are! What a price to pay! Seeing is believing. After you have experienced poor sportsmanship, you will, no doubt, begin to understand, even appreciate, the necessity for tennis etiquette.

● ● ●

My child's first tournament is coming up. What can I do to prepare my child mentally? What words of wisdom can I impart?

Explain that a tournament and each match are learning experiences. Your child is required to appear on time and is encouraged to have fun, to do his or her best and to learn from the experience.

There is no shame in losing. Remember that there can be only one player who wins the tournament, but there are many winners who have "given it their all." Also, remind your child that the winners of today may not always become the winners of tomorrow. Such words can truly encourage your child to "never give up."

Being nervous during a tournament is natural. Tell your child what a famous comedian once said: "I stopped being nervous after the first hour of my one-hour program." Humor eases tension!

● ● ●

What if a child is too exhausted or too ill to play his or her best and decides to "tank" the match? What would you say if he or she does not even try at all, quits and walks off the court?

Before they walk on the court, players have to make the decision as to whether they feel ready and able to begin a match. A player will prove nothing by being a hero and pushing him- or herself to play beyond physical limits. If someone's injury persists or an illness occurs during match play, it is best to stop immediately.

It is inexcusable, however, for players to quit in the middle of a match just because they are losing. Try avoiding the "poor me" routine, which is the attitude of a real loser.

If a child is too sick to play a match, claim a default due to illness. This way, your child can still walk away with head held high.

● ● ●

How can I, as a parent who knows little about tennis, be supportive of my child's tennis development?

Here are suggestions that will help you make a difference in showing your support:

- For starters, it is important to provide the opportunity for your child to enjoy tennis in the first place. Find out where tennis programs are offered, discuss having fun while playing and enroll your child with his or her friends, if possible.

- Provide your child with transportation to the court, outfit him or her in proper tennis attire and obtain tennis literature from the library, bookstore or the USTA.

- Consider this a special opportunity to get to know each other better and to share both feelings and attitudes about tennis, sports and life in general.

- Give your child endless encouragement. Help him or her to understand the meaning of "Rome wasn't built in a day" while you explain that good tennis players are never made overnight.

- Learn the language of tennis. Know the rules, how the score is kept and who the present tennis stars are.

- Show interest in what your child learns in class and learn why some skills are difficult to master. Ask the pro how you can help to reinforce the lessons he or she is trying to teach.

- Also, investigate how your child can earn extra money for lessons and tournaments, as well as for equipment and clothing. Your financial support is important.

- Proudly keep a scrapbook of your child's tournament results.

- Expose your child to professional tournaments and quality local players, as well as to tennis events that are be aired on television or cable television.

- Without hindering your child's other responsibilities, including schoolwork and other obligations, give him or her the opportunity, as well as the encouragement, to practice. Practice can make a game excellent, if not perfect.

TENNIS GREATS SPEAK OUT

Ashley Cooper

International Tennis Hall of Famer. Ranked number one in the world two years in a row. Winner of many singles and doubles titles, including Wimbledon (singles), the U.S. Open (singles and doubles), the French Open (doubles 2X) and the Australian Open (singles 2X and doubles).

Tennis etiquette and playing within the rules of our great game go hand in hand. A breakdown of either begins to demean the sport.

One aspect has become very clear to me in 20 years of operating a large coaching program in Bisbane: a player who abuses etiquette and rules attracts media attention and a certain notoriety. However, no parent wants their child to behave in a similar manner.

Colin Dibley

Winner of many singles and doubles titles, including the World Championship Tennis Tournament at La Costa, Calif. Ranked number one in the world in the Men's 35 singles three years in a row. Member of the Australian Davis Cup Team. Known for his world record serve clocked at over 148 mph.

Tennis etiquette is having respect for your opponents, as well as being able to compete hard against them. It is a fine balance, which must be accomplished to achieve your full potential and to have the respect of your fellow players.

It also encompasses the treatment that you extend to players on adjacent courts, because many times on a recreational level, the courts are side by side and not divided by fences. I also believe that pros and parents should teach children tennis etiquette at an early age so that it just becomes second nature.

Jonathan Exley

Evonne Goolagong

International Tennis Hall of Famer. Winner of many singles and doubles titles, including Wimbledon (singles 2X and doubles), the French Open (singles and mixed doubles), the Australian Open (singles and doubles 4X). Finished in the world's top ten in singles nine years.

Tennis etiquette is important. I am out there on the court not just to inspire young kids to play this wonderful healthy sport, but to inspire good character and good patience, as well as sportsmanship. These qualities, I find, many people remember even after finishing the pro tour. It is something that carries you through the rest of your life.

These days I try to teach my kids the same qualities that will carry them through their lives, and I remind them to keep smiling.

Rod Laver

International Tennis Hall of Famer. Ranked number one in the world four years. Winner of many singles and doubles titles, including Wimbledon (singles 4X, doubles and mixed doubles 2X), the U.S. Open (singles 2X), the French Open (singles 2X, doubles and mixed doubles) and the Australian Open (singles 3X and doubles 4X). The only two-time Grand Slam winner.

Most Australians are taught early on that practicing sportsmanship and etiquette comes before winning. Parents certainly have the responsibility of making sure their children understand this, regardless of which sport they play.

Competition and winning are healthy and rewarding at all levels of the game. Also, it is important to acknowledge how an opponent feels after a loss. It is up to you as a player to show your opponent respect by a firm handshake and condolences. This kind of response sets the stage for many enjoyable matches in the future, along with helping you to make lasting friendships.

Helena Sukova

Winner of many singles and doubles titles, including Wimbledon (doubles 4X and mixed doubles 3X), the U.S. Open (doubles 2X and mixed doubles), the French Open (doubles and mixed doubles) and the Australian Open (doubles 2X). Finished in the world's top ten in singles six years. Czech Republic Federation Cup Player.

When I was a little girl, I used to look up to my mother, who I always thought was a great example to many people and showed what etiquette on the tennis court and in daily life should be. As I grew older, I had the opportunity to see many other great tennis stars in person and on the court. I have always admired and tried to imitate the ones that not only produced the right shots at the right time, but also displayed sportsmanship and good character.

Since these players have made a great difference in my understanding of the game, I have tried to do the same by passing along the right message that was given to me.

photo: Tom Dyer

Peter Burwash International tennis professionals from around the world

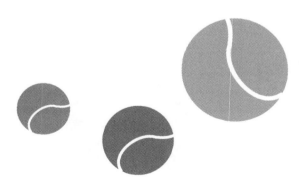

The Zen of Tennis

CHAPTER EIGHT

Tips for Teaching Professionals

Tips for Teaching Professionals

The greatest pleasure in tennis comes from a knowledge and comprehension of the game, what we as teaching professionals should aim to develop in our clients. By being good role models and properly guiding students in the basics of the game, we can convey and thus pass on a sense of the same love and joy tennis claims as its legacy.

It is also important that we professionals try to teach the finer points of tennis that go beyond the basic rules and discuss the proper protocols of tennis etiquette. If an instructor adheres to the following guidelines, I can assure you that clients not only will flock to his or her classes but also will get much more out of their practice sessions. Of even greater importance is the sustained satisfaction that your students will enjoy because of their positive tennis experience. A lot depends on us pros.

Professional Responsibilities

1. Act professionally on the court at all times and at all costs. Students look up to you as the example on and off the courts. You are responsible for guiding their actions and developing their attitude within the realm of the sport. Most assuredly, this guidance includes the protocols of tennis etiquette. I find it helpful to illustrate proper responses and etiquette with actual court situations that may arise.

   You will find that teaching tennis etiquette is just as important as teaching a good forehand. We need both in order to get along in the game of tennis at all levels of play.

2. Never take advantage of your position by welcoming amorous reactions from clients. It is very easy for students to become infatuated with their instructor. So, aim to keep your work on a professional level and avoid all cause for suspicion.

3. Treat all clients with equal respect. All adults and children are to be treated similarly. While the terminology of your teaching will vary, the respect must always remain constant. As a professional and a leader, remember that you set the standard.

4. As a teaching professional, you are primarily responsible for controlling the behavior of your students on and around the court. This rule applies to both young people and adults, who are capable of being just as loud, boisterous and disruptive.

   Poor behavior is like a virus; if overlooked, it only gets worse. Besides disrupting your teaching and also your clients' learning, it hampers the play of others nearby.

   If a young student misbehaves, it is wise to take him or her aside privately (away from his or her peers) and explain the seriousness of his or her actions. If the behavioral problem persists, a telephone call to the youngster's parents usually brings results.

5. Be sure that you know the rules yourself. You are not required to memorize them, but be familiar with them. Unless the situation is something very technical, have the basic rules in your head and keep a copy in your tennis bag.

6. Make a mental checklist of any additional items you might need before you begin your day of tennis lessons. Include in your general list the following supplies: a can of new balls, a large ball hopper to hold practice balls, bottled water, tow-

els, a couple of spare racquets (in case you or your client pops a string), your appointment book, a pen or pencil, extra shirts, a headband, a handful of wristbands, a high SPF sunblock, a sun visor, sunglasses and a medical emergency kit, which includes insect repellent.

Feel free to add to this list based on your needs and experience. I find it advantageous to keep my cellular phone close at hand for my students' use or for last-minute cancellations and emergencies.

7. If an emergency arises or you are ill and are forced to cancel a lesson, either you or someone acting on your behalf should contact your client as soon as possible. Keep your client's home and work numbers on file and in your tennis bag. Besides being convenient, this practice shows your client what a well-organized person you are. Also, be sure to reschedule each time a lesson is canceled.

8. Inclement weather always presents a problem. Discuss procedures and follow up with proper communication, since the weather can play havoc with schedules. Direct cancellations are far better than assumptions for all concerned.

9. Be cognizant of safety during lessons, especially when you teach young people or groups. A reckless swing can easily meet another student before it meets the ball. You need to be knowledgeable about emergency treatment for problems such as cuts and bruises and, if needed, cardiovascular resuscitation. Know whom to call and where to go in an emergency. Keep vital phone numbers readily available.

10. Help clients to avoid getting overheated or dehydrated. Encourage them to drink plenty of water not only on hot days but whenever possible, including court changeovers. If the club or the court has no water cooler, bring your own bottled water. Another advantage: Water breaks provide a

good opportunity to discuss your student's stroke or game.

11. Apparel also plays an important role for an instructor. Set the example by appearing professional and wearing proper tennis attire. You will feel better if you change sweaty clothes often throughout the day. Needless to say, bathing suit tops and cut-offs are not considered acceptable.

    It is all right to promote supplier outfits and shoes, as long as you are sincere in endorsing their quality and performance. On occasion, I have seen well-established pros pass on their old equipment and attire to needy students.

12. While taking lessons, clients often share personal thoughts, secrets and feelings. As a professional, you need to keep these disclosures in strict confidence.

13. When giving a lesson, be conscious of errant balls. Also, try to keep voice levels down as much as you can so as not to interrupt or distract players on nearby courts.

14. Keep a keen eye on the quality of your practice balls. The best way to get shoulder and arm injuries is by using old tennis balls. How embarrassing it would be for you to be told by a client, "Your practice balls are too old." Do a good deed by giving the old balls to the junior player program at a local club or to a nearby school.

15. When teaching young people, regularly communicate with parents about their children's progress and behavior. It is helpful to suggest what you would like the parents to work on if they practice with their child. Such feedback helps to get the parents interested and involved, which makes them feel that their money is well spent.

16. Tennis instructors, like all professionals, already receive

their fair share of abuse from others. They certainly do not need another instructor making it worse. So never put down another pro or the profession and definitely never a client. It is important to demonstrate respect for yourself and others at all times.

By respecting other pros, we are more likely to promote tennis as a sport that unites people, rather than separating them. I have even gone so far as to recommend that a client work with another coach whose teaching style best suited their style of game.

17. At times during our career, we tennis pros are faced with the opportunity to help others without monetary compensation. Call it "pay-back time" for the good we have received from the sport that we love. While it might not be something we want to advertise, it comes from that urge to help others.

When I see young people recklessly swinging racquets, I go over to their court and ask if I could show them some simple ways to improve their stroke. Many simply cannot afford lessons from a pro. I believe that it is a moral obligation for pros to try to help. If you prefer not to give these players free lessons, why not at least give them a reasonable discount or explain where they can get less expensive instruction?

Who the coach is does not matter as long as they are learning to play and enjoy tennis as the lifetime sport it is intended to be.

Winning Teaching Tactics

1. Teach in a way that works best for each student. Find out what is the best motivator for that individual. Some will learn best by having a stroke physically illustrated, while others tend to understand things better through a technical explanation.

Many words suit some; few words suit others. Repetition of key words works best for almost anyone. It can be a trial-and-error process with each student. Even if the process becomes boring, it is your responsibility to avoid a dry and humdrum atmosphere and to create an enjoyable atmosphere throughout the lesson.

2. I have heard about many gurus who teach nothing but love—love for oneself and others and love of everything imaginable. In a similar way, we pros should teach love for the game of tennis. Isn't it always the case that a person who loves what he or she is doing is also highly successful at it? If you help students enjoy the practice sessions and those with whom they play, they will invariably come to love and appreciate the game more. Net result? A winner.

3. During a lesson, be relaxed and have patience. This demeanor will help your clients to acquire the same relaxed and patient attitude, whether practicing or playing a match. Also, if you keep the lesson geared to their skill level, it will tend to make them feel more comfortable and content with their overall performance.

4. Draw out your clients' goals. Determine whether they just want to have a good workout or are hoping to win the club championship or to compete on a national level.

5. Focus on improving your clients' weaknesses and on building their strengths. Both are essential for confidence.

6. Remember, how students learn is as important as what they learn. Likewise, how the pro teaches is just as important as what he or she teaches. Yelling, screaming, demeaning and intimidating are definite no-no's. Embarrassing a player because of his or her performance or conduct is a fast way to lose clients and get them to dislike the game. Make sure

that your students always leave the court on a positive note, eager to return for another lesson.

7. Having fun and enjoying a sport are enhanced by showing a good sense of humor. So always incorporate humor into the lesson and promote laughter around the court, which will put a damper on tension and stress. Humor is a panacea in sports and life that can make losing a match or going through life's tribulations a bit more bearable.

8. When it is a bad day, modify your lessons by setting up more drills and accentuating fun on the court. You could introduce your students to trick or fun shots that you both can laugh about. Tell them about the difficulty of achieving the between-the-legs stroke while running away from the net or the behind-the-back tap over the net shot, which is so exciting to watch the pros do with great ease.

    Your client is paying good money to learn and have fun and certainly looks forward to seeing you and enjoying the lesson. Do not take that ugly mood of yours out on him or her. Repeat the phrase "The show must go on" and keep that broad smile on your face.

9. Sometimes, your student's entire game will need revamping. Do not overwhelm him or her with a complete makeover. Instead, develop a long-term program and work on one thing at a time.

    Stay within the realm of simple basics, working within your student's own individual style. Teach technically correct principles in a way that matches your student's comfort level and natural ability. It is amazing to realize how many unique styles flourish among the top pros on the major circuit, yet they all have developed within their own comfort and ability zones.

10. Praise is essential for motivation and morale. Being posi tive rather than negative helps to stimulate fun and enthusiasm

in an exhausted student. Your encouragement can go a long way.

11. Discourage feelings of self-pity and the dumb-excuse attitude in tennis. I cannot help but smile when I hear the "poor me" excuses offered by a student for a terrible performance on the court: "I had a bad draw in the tournament," or "The line calls were against me," or "My opponent was just lucky today."

    Teach students to accept obstacles as they occur and to enjoy the learning process. I cannot think of a famous professional who has a perfect all-wins-and-no-loss record. So, let's try to turn those negative experiences into positive future results.

12. Evaluate how hard your students want to be pushed both mentally and physically during a lesson. Most likely, they will not be in as good a physical condition as you are. Especially for beginners, keep the lessons simple and avoid overwhelming them with complicated pointers.

13. I like to stress to my students, "Pay less attention to the score and more attention to your game." Teach your students to stay focused on their game by stressing the importance of worrying less about winning points and paying more attention to mastering their strokes, correcting bad habits, using good judgment and strategy and always displaying good tennis etiquette.

    Think about it. They feel great (good attitude), they are playing their best game (comfortable with their strokes), and they are having fun in the process (good etiquette). So help them learn how to concentrate on the game rather than on the score. They not only will improve but also will enjoy their game a lot more.

14. I also find it obligatory to teach my students the Yogi Berra adage, "It ain't over til it's over!" There is an almost end-

less list of examples of a player being down two match points and coming back to win, as if miraculously. That "never say die" attitude is what makes champions out of mediocre players.

15. Even pros commit errors. For one day last year, I know I really was perfect, but before and after that I admit that I have made mistakes. Never be ashamed to admit your error. Also, students should never take the blame for balls that are so wide that they are unreachable or too overpowering. Frankly, your being more human will make your students feel better and will keep everyone more relaxed.

16. Avoid being a show-off, unless it is the best way to illustrate what you are trying to teach. Hitting aces or passing shots against students serves only to induce discouragement at best. Students expect you to be good. More importantly, they expect you to teach them how to become proficient tennis players, even to the point that someday they could beat you on the court.

17. Try not to repeat the same thing over and over again, unless you enjoy sounding like a parrot. Teaching with enthusiasm at all levels of play (beginner, intermediate and advanced) and with all ages (6, 18, 40 or 80) can help to make your students enthusiastic. They will want to return to your class to learn more because you have made it fun for them to learn despite the hard work.

18. During the lesson, make it a habit to ask your student if he or she is able to hear you. Many times, halfway through a lesson, I have stopped to ask a question and discovered that the student could not hear me and was too embarrassed to ask me to repeat what I had said. So, it is important at the beginning of each drill that you explain the exercise, indicate what the intended goal is and ask if the student has any questions.

19. Carefully avoid making any rash observations or promises about a client's progress. The most honest and safest thing you could say is, "Almost everything within your physical limits is possible with enough practice and desire."

20. It is a good habit to close each lesson by asking your students whether they have any questions about what you have covered that day. I often find that they are too shy or embarrassed to admit they did not understand something. So "ask and you shall receive" answers and faster improvement in your student's game.

21. Stress to your students how important it is to give an opponent the benefit of the doubt on close line calls, both in the beginning of a game and even at match point. Instill pride and honor, which they also will carry with them away from the court.

22. Encourage students to acknowledge an opponent's good shot, in addition to their own. A clenched fist can be a positive way to reinforce confidence and affirm your student's ability to make a good shot. Be positive and sincere during play to help keep the atmosphere on the court light and pleasant for everyone.

23. Avoid any show of favoritism to any individual in a group setting. You may have to modify your program due to the ability of certain players in the group, but it is necessary to make them all feel equally important. All of my students deserve some compliment during a lesson, even if it is only for attentiveness and effort.

TENNIS GREATS SPEAK OUT

Peter Burwash

Peter Burwash in one of the best coaches in the game. He has been founder and president of Peter Burwash International for 27 years. PBI is the world's largest tennis management company, operating in 32 countries at the most beautiful resorts you could ever imagine. His staff of teaching professionals (see photo on page 196) has a reputation for giving first-class service and quality instruction.

The Protocols of Being a Good Teaching Professional

Tennis professionals who have the good fortune to teach are extremely lucky, as we have an amazing gift to give people. The Gift of Tennis. How many sports can people play socially and competitively into their 90s?

The biggest challenge a tennis professional has is to not try to teach their students in the mold that they themselves played. Every player has a unique style and a unique learning process. This is why I do not agree with teaching systems. It is important for each professional to teach individuals.

It helps if a teaching professional has had to struggle with learning the game as he/she grew up. This allows for two important aspects. First, they understand the struggle and can be empathetic with their student. And secondly, they invariably have a better understanding of the game.

A number of years ago in Hawaii, I took my daughter, who was five at the time, skating. We got on the ice and she asked me to teach her how to skate. I thought and thought and thought. When I was three, I skated almost naturally within the first hour. There was no struggle at all. It came easily. The end result is I haven't got a clue how to teach a person how to skate.

On the other hand, absolutely nothing came easily for me in tennis. And I have been teaching the sport for over 30 years now. And I love teaching as much today as I did when I had my first lesson.

So many teaching professionals have told me over the years that they no longer want to teach tennis because it is boring. I tell them that teaching tennis is not boring but *you* are boring. The most important part of being a teaching professional is that you have to love *teaching* and *sharing*. If you don't have the passion for those two, then you will never be a good teacher.

If you are enthusiastic, then people will want to come to see you. There are so many appointments people don't want to have (doctors, dentists, cars, etc.) that their tennis lesson is often the bright moment in their day. So tennis professionals must do everything they can to make it the best hour of the day for each student.

And finally, a teaching professional must have the most important ingredient of *humility*. Good teachers understand we are there to serve the student, not control them. Students don't want to hear how you won the under 16 sectional championships multi-years ago. Good teachers focus their energy on the student, not themselves.

Teaching is a privilege and an honor. Teaching tennis is an incredible profession. For those of us that have had the chance to help those students enjoy the game even more, we thank you and hope you will be playing in the over 90 championships someday.

Shirley Fry-Irvin

International Tennis Hall of Famer. Ranked number one in the world. Winner of many singles and doubles titles, including Wimbledon (singles, doubles 3X and mixed doubles), the U.S. Open (singles and doubles 4X), the French Open (singles and doubles 4X) and the Australian Open (singles and doubles).

Tennis etiquette is just as important as any rules of decorum in any of life's endeavors.

My father truly believed in the lessons learned from participating in all sports. It not only promoted our physical well-being but also our social well-being. Play by the rules and respect, acceptance and friendly rivalry would follow. From the age of 9 to 21, I traveled to tennis tourneys alone. You could say I learned from many families the etiquette expected on the court, as a guest in a home, as a representative of my country abroad.

I could not say my thoughts on this subject any better than my fellow Ohioan, Billy Talbert, did. I have never forgotten the lines of Rudyard Kipling at Wimbledon: "If you can meet with Triumph and Disaster and treat those two imposters just the same," or the quote from Grantland Rice at Forest Hills: "It matters not if you win or lose but how you play the game."

Words can be as inspiring as actions. I truly value my Sportsmanship Awards as much as any Grand Slam Titles.

Russ Adams

Owen Davidson

Top doubles specialist. Winner of many singles and doubles titles, including Wimbledon (mixed doubles 4X), the U.S. Open (doubles and mixed doubles 4X), the French Open (mixed doubles) and the Australian Open (doubles and mixed doubles 2X). Australian Davis Cup player.

As a player I was taught at a very young age by Harry Hopman the importance of etiquette and sportsmanship in our great game of tennis.

Tennis is very much a one-against-one personality contest, and much of the "real" character of a person is openly displayed under stress on the tennis court.

I believe that out of respect for all the great players of the past who tried so hard to make this game stronger with little or no reward, it is our job to show respect for our opponents today by maintaining courtesy and etiquette at the highest level. Starting with the way we dress on court ("if you can't be a great tennis player you can at least look like one") to our behavior toward the opponent, the officials, the sponsors, and the public, we have an obligation to uphold the standards of the game at all times.

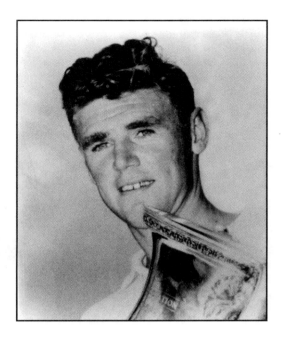

Frank Sedgman

International Tennis Hall of Famer. Ranked number one in the world two years in a row. Winner of many singles and doubles titles, including Wimbledon (singles, doubles 3X and mixed doubles 2X), the U.S. Open (singles 2X, doubles 2X and mixed doubles 2X), the French Open (doubles 2X and mixed doubles 2X) and the Australian Open (singles 2X, doubles 2X and mixed doubles 2X)

I was taught tennis etiquette by my peers, including Jack Crawford, Harry Hopman and Gerald Patterson. During my career, I have found that having good manners, good sportsmanship and a good temperament can mean the difference between winning and losing on many an occasion. More importantly, once you have finished your career, you are treated with respect for your past achievements.

Left: Michel Bergerac
Southampton, N.Y.

Right: Dr. Lilly Chen
New York, N.Y.

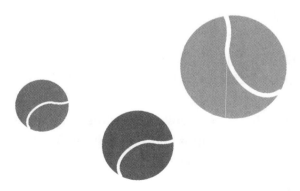

CHAPTER NINE
Spectator Savvy

Spectator Savvy

Etiquette is as important for spectators as it is for players. The way you behave as a spectator will affect everyone around you. So try to be considerate of the other spectators as well as the players you are watching.

I find it commendable that the golf galleries respect the golfer as he or she is about to swing at the ball. At the instant the golfer addresses the ball, a hush permeates the crowd. The atmosphere is pure silence until the club strikes that little white sphere. Some may think that the oohs and aahs are the spectators' gasping for air. Absolutely not. All savvy spectators know that the oohs and aahs are only a polite expression of their support.

Let's take note and learn from the following spectator situations.

With drinks in hand, a friend and I are enjoying a match in progress. The conversation turns to the fun activities of the previous evening. Suddenly I realize some people have been overhearing our remarks, because they start giving us nasty looks and a volley of "hushes." Did we do something wrong?

If within earshot range of a match, try to keep your conversation to a whisper. Loud talking, laughter and excessive motions can distract players when they are trying to concentrate. You need not go to an extreme by being totally quiet or a motionless mummy, but wild waving to others is a no-no. Be considerate and use your own discretion. When you respect the players and the other spectators, you are allowing others to enjoy the game.

I am trying to watch an important match, but am constantly being disturbed by people walking in front of me. They could just as easily walk behind. Why don't they use their common sense?

It is true that people will sometimes be oblivious to their own surroundings. I think the best you can do without purposely tripping someone is to position yourself out of other people's way. As always, it is important to set a good example yourself.

● ● ●

I start watching an exciting match between two good players when suddenly they begin arguing over "in" and "out" balls and the score. Unexpectedly, they turn to me for an answer. What should I say?

It is unfair for you or any spectator to voice an opinion on any line call. Unless you have been asked to referee the entire match or have been given the authority to be a linesman or umpire, never get directly involved. It is a no-win situation and unfair to all parties.

● ● ●

I'm playing an important match, the finals for the club championship. My opponent has brought along his entire family and all the friends he could muster. For every point my opponent wins, the fans go wild, screaming and applauding even the shots I hit into the net, including my double faults! I pray to hit a winning shot because that is the only time that the crowd keeps quiet. Where are people's manners? Does competition have to be so ugly?

It is unfortunate when anyone falls victim to poor sportsmanship. We can do little about it without falling to that same level. I contend, your best reaction is to block out the noise and pretend the cheering from the gallery is for you. Stay focused on the ball and beat the trousers off your opponent. As for your friends who may be at the match to watch, try to make them aware of good etiquette as spectators and suggest that they set the tone for the others.

Personally, I like telling my opponent "great shot" when there is honest justification. It not only motivates me but also makes him or her feel good, and I know that he or she would like to try that shot over again. Next time, however, my opponent may not be as lucky.

● ● ●

I'm playing an important club match at which a baby won't stop crying. What does tennis etiquette have to say about spectators bringing babies to a match? I'm sure this distraction disturbs others, too.

Without causing too much commotion, politely inform the adult or the person caring for the baby of your problem. It is then up to that individual to quiet the baby or take the child away from the match until there is no longer a distraction.

When in doubt, one can defer to Wimbledon standards, which include "no small infants."

TENNIS GREATS
SPEAK OUT

Vic Braden

Internationally known instructor, analyst and commentator.
Winner of the United States Tennis Association's Tennis Education
Merit Award for contributing the most to tennis in America.
Recipient of the United States Professional Tennis Association
Coach of the Year Award and the Orange County Hall of Fame
Lifetime Achievement Award.

Respect must be earned. In 1974, in a World Championship final in Dallas, Texas, Arthur Ashe hit a great shot against Stan Smith. The crowd thought the ball was in. Thousands of dollars were riding on the call. The linesman called the ball out. The crowd went berserk. Arthur turned to Stan Smith and said, "Was the ball out?" Stan answered, "Yes." There was no question from Arthur. Stan's etiquette and ethics were trusted 100 percent by Arthur. Two points were made here. Arthur trusted Stan and Stan had earned the trust over many years. Tennis etiquette lasts for a lifetime.

Rosie Casals

International Tennis Hall of Famer. Winner of many singles and doubles titles, including Wimbledon (doubles 5X, mixed doubles 2X) and the U.S. Open (doubles 4X and mixed doubles). Finished in the world's top ten in singles 12 years in a row.

Tennis etiquette is important because it shows respect for the rules of tennis, as well as for your opponents and your partner.

Tim Mayotte

Winner of many singles and doubles titles, including a silver medal in the Olympics. Finished in the world's top ten in singles two years in a row. U.S. Davis Cup player.

Mats Wilander was one of the great champions of the modern era, a fact that I do not hear often enough. Wilander upheld the highest standards of consideration for the rules of the game and his fellow players. One incident clearly exemplifies this.

Wilander, only seventeen, was playing Jose Luis Clerc in the semi's of the French Open in 1982. To appreciate the magnitude of this, it is important to remember that Wilander was on the verge of making it to his first Grand Slam final. It was match point for Wilander.

A ground stroke Clerc hit close to the line was ruled out and would have given Wilander the win in the four-hour match. Before an instant passed, however, Wilander had overruled the linesperson and had called to replay the point.

Wilander, of course, went on to win the match and his first Grand Slam title. I will never forget how calmly and matter-of-factly he reacted in that situation and how he risked losing his chance at the French Open to do what he thought was right.

Perhaps my own most personally enriching experience came in a match I played against Kevin Curren on Centre Court at Wimbledon in 1983. As the match was progressing, I felt something special (for lack of a better word) was developing. At the beginning of the final set, the sun broke through the clouds for the first time that day and cast a long shaft of light across the grass. Centre Court seemed to be glowing, while the tennis game seemed to respond to the setting.

We both had served and returned well and often. The winners were outnumbering the errors. Stretch volleys and passing shots punctuated every game. Kevin finally put me away in the fourth set with a winning serve. After match point, while approaching the net to shake his hand, I began to clap. It was a spontaneous gesture. On some level, I must have wanted to show my appreciation for all the things that had made up that match, including the setting, Kevin's sportsmanship, the quality of the tennis and the crowd's involvement.

My clapping touched a lot of spectators for whatever reason. It was very gratifying to know that others had gotten some satisfaction from my expression of etiquette.

Ross Case

Top doubles specialist. Winner of many singles and doubles titles, including Wimbledon (doubles) and the Australian Open (doubles). Australian Davis Cup player.

I believe tennis etiquette is essential for the well-being of the game. A player can be competitive and tough on the court and can still demonstrate good sportsmanship. Tennis etiquette, sportsmanship, toughness and competitiveness are also for the spectators and bring more people out to watch and more players to play the game.

Tennis professional Wendy Brown with student
Domenica "Nikki" Digiacomo

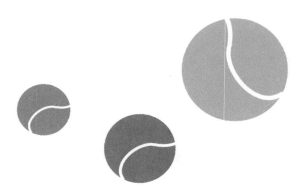

CHAPTER TEN

The Future of Tennis

What kind of court situation might tennis players of the future have to look forward to? With my eyes closed and my mind open, I can envision the following scenario:

- Court nets that recoil when your allotted time has expired.

- Soundproofing between courts.

- Cameras on every court to monitor behavior.

- Holograms that utilize computer images in place of individuals that you play against at your club or home court.

- Air curtains that prevent errant balls from going onto adjacent courts and disturbing other players.

- Magnetic ball retrievers that will clear the court as well as return balls to the server.

- Magnetic line callers that sense and call balls "out" when they land outside their magnetic field.

- A special composition tennis ball that will retain its playability and firmness for up to five years.

- Internally heated court surfaces that can dry in minutes and automatically modulate a comfortable court temperature.

- Automatic lie-detector tests at net posts to determine honesty in questionable calls (such as double bounces).

Although the future is perhaps difficult, even impossible, to imagine, remember that "today's dream is tomorrow's reality." Before assuming a doom and gloom scenario, let us step back with

a new awareness and optimism and reflect on how tennis has benefited people's lives and how its enriching heritage will help sustain
the foundation for its popularity and success in the future.

Tennis, which began as a graceful, civilized sport for ladies and
gentlemen, brought people together to socialize and have fun. A
great shot was thrilling, regardless of who hit it. The exhilarating
lunges and leaps, as well as the beautiful "pock" sound of the tennis ball hitting the strings, were pleasant to players and spectators
alike. It was taken for granted that everyone was a good sport, and
most were. Tennis attire was simple and subdued and served its purpose. Best of all, it was obvious that, whether playing or watching,
everyone was having a good time and enjoying a nice, healthy balance of competition and fun.

Through the years I have observed a decline of enjoyment in tennis among our youth, a trend I find very disconcerting. With the rig-
ors of school and peer pressure, it is important that young people
have an outlet to enjoy themselves and alleviate their pent-up stress.
Often, students become easily frustrated and demand instant
improvement from lessons and practice. This feeling of frustration
creates an uncomfortable atmosphere, not only for the stressed student and other players on or near the court but especially for the tennis pro who is trying his or her best to build the student's self-confidence and teach proper mechanics.

Even social playing has become dominated by the view that you
are expected to "beat" your opponent. The basic desire to practice
has been changed to a striving force to become master on the court.
Whereas basketball players customarily say, "Let's shoot some bas-
kets" or golfers join in a round of golf, tennis players will challeng-
ingly say, "Let's play a set against each other."

This type of attitude among older and younger players inevitably
undercuts enjoyment, entertainment and relaxation. Keep in mind
that tennis is a sport, defined as "a form of amusement or of fun or

of play." Even though tennis is my profession, I initially pursued it for the purposes of physical recreation and enjoyment. The intended goal of the game is to complement our lives with a pleasant detour from everyday activities, including work, not to contribute to stress, anger and frustration. In this book, I have directed my comments to the recreational and amateur players of tennis. It is within these amateur ranks that the survival of tennis as a sport will prevail, just as was originally intended years ago. All of us can help make a difference.

Few young players will ever break into the ranks of tomorrow's top professionals, yet everyone certainly can benefit from the endless mental, social and physical enrichment to be enjoyed from this sport.

Every French teacher with whom I have ever studied emphasized that learning a language means little unless you make the effort to practice what you have learned. While learning tennis etiquette is important, it is much more important to practice it.

Every horseback-riding instructor has told me that when you fall off a horse, you must immediately get back on. Never lose self-confidence and control! The more time we spend practicing the protocols of tennis etiquette, the better we can become as players and the more deeply we will enjoy the game's many riches.

Through tennis etiquette, we can progress beyond prejudice in the areas of age, religion, race, sexuality and cultural background, accepting one another in the spirit of a common love—tennis. As we practice and teach the protocols of tennis etiquette and pass on the history and traditions that have made tennis so exciting and enjoyable, we will ensure that the sport continues its popularity into the future.

It may be obvious, but good experiences are among the best things that we can have and can look forward to in life. Practicing tennis etiquette in whatever situation you find yourself will also bring you a lot of good experiences. As you live by the ideals of fair play, courtesy and tennis protocol, you are sowing the seeds of a truly gratifying future.

Tennis has had an extraordinary past filled with idealism and many beautiful memories for those fortunate enough to be part of it. Even if we have not had an opportunity to share in that magnificent history, we can still reap its benefits by practicing tennis etiquette, which will thus create a new legacy that continues to replicate the glory of tennis.

I recall the many professionals I observed during my short professional career who proudly exemplified tennis etiquette by letting their ability speak louder than a complaining voice. My own "Etiquette Hall of Fame" would include as its members all the players who have contributed to my book as well as to the game of tennis, not only through their outstanding record of achievement but also through their exemplary adherence to proper tennis etiquette. My "Etiquette Hall of Famers" would also include beginners through advanced players, parents, children of all ages, and everyone who has wanted to play, enjoy and share in the fun of this exhilarating sport. Isn't it refreshing to know that tennis can have such a variety of lifetime winners, regardless of the score?

So the next time you are on the tennis court, why not ask yourself, "Am I practicing tennis etiquette? Am I being fair, honest and respectful to everyone as well as myself?" Perhaps if we all try to answer these questions in the affirmative, we will destroy the possibility of human beings playing against a lifeless hologram that speaks in a hollow voice: *"You have double-faulted again....you should be ashamed of yourself!"* A future occurrence such as this would erase the beauty and certainly the pleasure of tennis.

The Zen of Tennis is really a philosophy that is essential to success not only on the tennis court but also in your everyday life. It is about learning from your mistakes and not giving the bad days so much significance. If we relax and enjoy the process, we cannot help but succeed, for the process will become its own reward.

I guarantee that as you practice tennis etiquette, you will experience greater triumphs and fewer disappointments both on and off the court. Most of all, the sense of pride and accomplishment you feel will truly become your winning ticket to happiness and success.

TENNIS GREATS SPEAK OUT

Nick Bollettieri

Nick has coached more kids to stardom than any other tennis pro in the world. He is the president and founder of the Bollettieri Tennis Academy. After coaching tennis for more than 45 years, he was named the United States Olympic Committee National Coach of the Year in 1999 by the USTA. In the same year he also received the International Tennis Hall of Fame Education Merit Award.

I've been building the future of tennis at the Bollettieri Tennis Academy for several decades. My focus with these young children is to prepare them not only for the demands of their tennis life but also the challenges of life itself.

Charles M. Pasarell, Jr.

Winner of many singles and doubles titles, including the U.S. National Indoors, Memphis, Tenn. (singles 2X and doubles). Formerly ranked number one in the U.S. Awarded the William Johnston trophy for outstanding character and etiquette on the tennis court.

We have witnessed great changes in the sport of tennis over the past 25 to 30 years, such as Open Championships with enormous prize-money purses; from wood to metal, from metal to graphite oversized, high-tech racquets; the tiebreaker scoring system and so on. However, one thing that has not changed and should never change is the tradition of shaking hands with one's opponent at the conclusion of a match.

While tennis is most definitely a very competitive athletic endeavor, it is still a game and a sport played fairly by gentlemen and ladies.

Tom Gullikson

Winner of many singles and doubles titles, including the U.S. Open (mixed doubles). Former coach of the U.S. Davis Cup team. Winner of the Miller-Lite International Tennis Hall of Fame Championships in Newport, R.I.

Tennis etiquette is important because it helps to build character in our players. The concepts of good sportsmanship and fair play carry over into everyday life as well.

Neale Fraser

International Tennis Hall of Famer. Ranked number one in the world two times. Winner of many singles and doubles titles, including Wimbledon (singles, doubles 2X and mixed doubles), the U.S. Open (singles 2X, doubles and mixed doubles 3X), the French Open (doubles 3X) and the Australian Open (doubles 3X and mixed doubles).

We all play the game of tennis to improve our skills in this great sport, to have a little exercise, to meet and make friends and, for some, to represent our family, state or country at the competitive level. By playing our sport with a degree of etiquette, irrespective of the category in which we play, our great game can be enjoyed by our opponent(s), as well as ourselves.

Etiquette is so easy to master, so quick to learn and so simple to put into operation. With tennis etiquette, we can all enjoy our game as we've never enjoyed it before.

Fox Photos

Louise Brough Clapp

International Tennis Hall of Famer. Winner of many singles and doubles titles, including Wimbledon (singles 4X, doubles 5X and mixed doubles 4X), the U.S. Open (singles, doubles 12X and mixed doubles 4X), the French Open (doubles 3X) and the Australian Open (singles and doubles). Winner of the National Service Bowl awarded to women who have made most outstanding contributions to tennis.

Please, let us treat the game of tennis that we all love and respect with the manners, civility and dignity that it deserves, whether competing or spectating. This is a game we all hold dear and one that has given us so much. We should honor it with good behavior and proper etiquette.

F or when the great scorer comes,
    To write against your name:
He'll write not that you won or lost,
But how you played the game.

Grantland Rice